# Tess of the d'Urbervilles

## THOMAS HARDY

# Guide written by
# Claire Wright

## Series Editor: Stewart Martin

A Letts **uide**

Every effort has been made to trace copyright holders and to obtain their permission for the use of copyright material. The author and publishers will gladly receive information enabling them to rectify any reference or credit in subsequent editions.

First published 1994
Reprinted 1996

Letts Educational
Aldine House
Aldine Place
London W12 8AW

0181 740 2266

**Text** © Claire Wright 1995

**Typeset by** Jordan Publishing Design

**Text Design** Jonathan Barnard

**Cover and text illustrations** Hugh Marshall

**Graphic illustration** Hugh Marshall

Design © BPP (Letts Educational) Ltd

**British Library Cataloguing in Publication Data**
A CIP record for this book is available from the British Library

ISBN 1 85758 273 X

Printed and bound in Great Britain
by Ashford Colour Press Ltd, Gosport, Hants

Letts Educational is the trading name of BPP (Letts Educational) Ltd

# ■ Contents

# ■ Plot synopsis

### Phase One: The Maiden

In the village of Marlott, in rural Wessex, John Durbeyfield discovers he is descended from the once-great family of d'Urberville. Vain and irresponsible, he and his wife urge their daughter Tess – a pretty girl, set apart from the other villagers by her sensitivity and education – to claim kinship with a rich namesake nearby. Blaming herself for the death of their horse when she falls asleep at the reins, Tess reluctantly agrees to seek help for the family. Alec d'Urberville, an arrogant, sensual young man (and not a true d'Urberville), gives her work. Tess becomes the innocent and unwilling target of Alec's attentions, and at night in the woods, he seduces her.

### Phase Two: Maiden No More

Tess returns home to bear Alec's child. She feels acutely shamed by her 'ruin', despite the rough acceptance of the rural community. When her child becomes sick and dies, Tess resolves to leave the village.

### Phase Three: The Rally

Tess arrives at Talbothays farm, where she works as a dairymaid for the genial Mr Crick. Her workmates include Marian, Retty, Izz – and Angel Clare (whom she first saw, briefly, at the beginning of the novel). He stands out by his refinement: the son of a clergyman, he has rejected a Church career and social status, and embraced rural life. Tess seems his ideal of the natural, pure country girl. They fall in love, but Tess is tormented by guilt: haunted by reminders of her 'sin', forced to deceive Angel for fear of losing him, and aware that her friends also love him.

### Phase Four: The Consequence

Finally, Tess agrees to marry Angel. She tries to confess everything, but cannot: even a letter fails, by chance, to reach him. On their wedding night, Angel admits an affair in his own past, and Tess trustingly tells him her own story.

### Phase Five: The Woman Pays

Angel, deeply shocked, rejects Tess: she is not the same ideal woman that he loved. Tess resignedly accepts his wish to live apart, and returns home, but the shallowness of her family drives her away. Angel goes to Brazil, while Tess hides the truth of their separation and, supporting her family, grows desperate for work. She labours through a harsh winter at Flintcomb-Ash farm: a barren place, under a vindictive master. Unwilling to write to Angel, Tess finally goes for news to his parents at Emminster, but – overhearing scornful remarks by his brothers – loses heart. Turning back, she encounters a preacher: it is Alec d'Urberville.

## Phase Six: The Convert

Alec's religious conversion is shaken by meeting Tess again. He renews his attentions, insistently playing on Tess's sense of guilt and her family's needs. Tess sends a desperate appeal to Angel, who, matured by suffering, has already had a change of heart. But when John Durbeyfield dies, his family are suddenly homeless. Tess despairs of Angel's return, and there – seemingly everywhere – is Alec, offering to help.

## Phase Seven: Fulfilment

Angel has returned to seek Tess. He tracks her down to Sandbourne – too late: she is with Alec. In shame and anger, Tess kills Alec and flees with Angel, who finally stands by her. They hide in a deserted mansion for a week of fragile happiness. Discovered, they move on to Stonehenge where, at dawn, the police close in. Tess goes calmly – 'I am ready' – to her execution.

# The structure of the novel

The narrative is a straightforward chronological account, divided into 'phases' reflecting stages in Tess's experience. Each phase builds towards a critical turning point, resolved at the start of the next phase.

|  | *Begins with...* | *Ends with...* |
|---|---|---|
| The Maiden | News of ancestry | Alec raping Tess |
| Maiden No More | Tess pregnant | Tess resolving to leave |
| The Rally | Tess coming to Talbothays | Love acknowledged |
| The Consequence | Angel planning marriage | Tess's confession |
| The Woman Pays | Angel rejecting Tess | Tess meeting Alec again |
| The Convert | Alec pursuing Tess again | Tess weakening |
| Fulfilment | Angel returning | Tess's execution |

This framework creates an atmosphere of suspense, despite the powerful sense of inevitability in the novel.

**Journeys** form a pattern within the narrative: roads and landscapes mirror the changes in Tess's feelings and fortunes.

**Nature** adds the underlying cycle of the seasons: reflecting 'seasons' in Tess's life, yet ultimately indifferent to human struggles.

The **central relationships** also shape the narrative, as Tess learns 'the cruelty of lust and the fragility of love': abused by Alec and idealised by Angel, she is betrayed by both. There is a repeated cycle of courtship and abandonment (by Angel), seduction (by Alec) and escape (by Tess). Only one of the men features in the story at any time, but Hardy keeps us – and Tess – constantly aware of the other: the triangle is ever-present.

**Themes, symbols and images** provide further patterns. Echoes of the past and omens of the future enrich the narrative. Recurring motifs, such as colours, birds and costumes, link characters and events.

Some critics think all this contrived. Do you find such patterns obvious and intrusive – or do they give you a more subtle and complex perspective on the story?

**"By experience... we find out a short way by a long wandering."** (Chapter 15)

MARLOTT (Blackmoor Vale)
'Fertile and sheltered', 'muddy'

SPRING: Tess heart-whole at the May Day Dance

THE SLOPES (Trantridge)
'Everything looked like money'

EARLY SUMMER: Premature ripeness at The Slopes

Downhill drive

MARLOTT
Again

MARCH: Alec appears, John dies. Mass migration

Walk under
'steely stars'

FLINTCOMB-ASH again
FEBRUARY: 'peaceful', until Alec reappears
EARLY SPRING: hopes of Angel's return but bad news from Marlott

A weary
'plod'

EMMINSTER
'The quiet vicarage'

MIDWINTER: Tess turns back

A pilgrimage

KINGSBERE
'Half-dead hamlet'

APRIL: Tess's family at the d'Urberville vaults

SANDBOURNE
'A glittering novelty'

MAY: a false spring of hope Angel returns. Tess kills Alec

Contented walk
with Angel

BRAMHURST
'Happy house'

Tess and Angel together at last

THE CHASE
'Primaeval forest'

MARLOTT
Again

TALBOTHAYS (Froom Valley)
'verdant flatness,' clear water

Uphill climb

A pilgrimage

'from heavy
to light'

AUTUMN: The 'fall' of
Tess

LATE SUMMER: The Harvest
SPRING: (2 years on)

SUMMER: Love and courtship
TO WINTER: Marriage

FLINTCOMB-ASH
'A starve-acre place'

WELLBRIDGE 'Mouldy'
seat of the d'Urbervilles

TALBOTHAYS again
'The gold of the summer
picture was now grey'

MARLOTT again
'No place for her now'

WINTER: Tess deserted

MIDWINTER: Angel
rejects Tess

STONEHENGE
'Older than the d'Urbervilles'

WINTONCASTER

Final journey

into night

Tess arrested at dawn
'Now I am at home'

JULY: Tess executed
'The sun's rays smiling on pitilessly'

# Who's who in
## *Tess of the d'Urbervilles*

Tess

### Tess Durbeyfield

Tess is the heart of the novel: its power depends on our identification with her. She is the focal point of Hardy's exploration of various themes, and sometimes embodies the 'essence of woman'. Yet Tess is also a complex, fully-realised character.

Hardy subtitled the novel 'A Pure Woman' (to great controversy). 'Pure' can mean both 'chaste' and 'essential'. Tess embodies the ideal or 'essence' of woman, in her instinctive sensuality, her capacity to love and to suffer. (Ironically, Angel falsely idealises her for her supposed virginity.) But Tess is also a child, forced too early into womanhood. Her innocence and the purity of her heart remain essentially untouched by the 'sins' which, according to Hardy, affront 'accepted social law', not nature.

Tess is intensely physically attractive, in a way that suggests both freshness (which attracts the idealistic Angel) and luxuriance (appealing to the sensual Alec). She has large, innocent eyes above a 'pouted-up deep red mouth'. Her mother thinks Tess's face is her 'trump card', but it proves a curse: Tess later fears and rejects her treacherous attractiveness.

Tess is different. Hardy makes this point when we first see her as the only girl wearing a red ribbon. The observer's eye is always drawn to her. She has an elusive dignity which sets her apart from other country girls. Even within her family, she is isolated by her education and sensitivity, and so robbed of vital support from them.

Tess is impulsive, imaginative and acutely sensitive: 'a vessel of emotions rather than reasons', susceptible to forebodings and daydreams. Overlaid with the 'conventional aspect' of social and religious values, however, this sensitivity feeds a capacity for guilt. An exaggerated, imaginative sense of moral responsibility tortures Tess. It prompts the fatal 'loss of courage' which makes her deceive Angel and, later, fail to approach his parents. It renders her vulnerable to emotional blackmail, especially by Alec. Projecting her self-blame onto others (and even onto Nature), she feels constantly ashamed and insecure. Tess develops an obsession with crime and death (reinforced by her association with the colour red – splashed blood, painted judgements, thorned roses) which proves prophetic.

Believing herself undeserving of happiness, Tess resigns herself to the role of victim. Passive submission, to other people's wishes and to 'fate', is characteristic of her. Yet it also contains an element of pride: 'reckless acquiescence' – daring chance to do its worst – is a d'Urberville trait.

In fact, Tess has many strengths: pride, courage, resilience, practicality and independence. She insists on carrying her own burdens (despite adding to them by refusing help). She works (notably at Flintcomb-Ash) with great stoicism. She resists Alec, showing impulsive flashes of spirit to the point of violence. Through endurance, she learns 'moral courage'. At certain moments, such as the baptism of her dying child, she transcends her suffering with true dignity.

Tess also shows a vast capacity for positive emotions, such as compassion, generosity, hope, delight, trust, loyalty and love. She has the potential for happiness, but her story is a tragedy of 'might have beens'.

Hardy emphasises Tess's kinship with nature. She is linked with birds and animals; her life is set against the rural landscape; the seasons reflect her fortunes and her moods. Yet nature is ultimately impersonal: even Tess is dwarfed by the expanse of the land.

All this raises a very important question. Is Tess, like the birds and animals, the passive and uncomprehending victim of external forces? Or does she – by her own personality and choices – cause her own tragedy?

## Alec d'Urberville

Alec

Alec appears in the novel twice: both times, as seducer and ruiner of Tess's hopes. We tend to see him, therefore, in his formal role as villain, and as a balance to Angel Clare. Alec represents 'the cruelty of lust' and perhaps also the careless abuses of the modern age. However, like Satan, with whom he is identified, he presents himself in different guises – an element of role play which adds irony to the stereotype.

Alec at first seems the traditional villain of Victorian melodrama, with his swarthy features, curling moustaches and 'bold, rolling eye'. This is the 'handsome unpleasantness' of a young rake. He is self-centred and capricious, pursuing Tess, initially, in a spirit of pure self-gratification. An arrogant desire for mastery shows in the way he treats his horse, just as he will later try to 'break' Tess.

Yet his forcefulness has a sensual quality that confuses her: she later confesses that she was dazzled. The account of the rape (or seduction?) is curiously ambivalent. Moreover, Alec shows genuine affection for Tess, and a willingness to take financial responsibility for her. He is refreshingly self-aware, freely admitting that he is 'a bad fellow'.

In his second incarnation, Alec is briefly 'The Convert', an ironic symbol of the failure of faith in the modern world. His conversion is unconvincing, but Alec's character throughout is consistent: capricious in taking the faith, passionate beneath the surface piety, and opportunistic in blaming Tess for his backsliding. The obviousness of his villainy now hides more subtle dangers: he plays relentlessly on Tess's loneliness and anxiety about her family. Yet his obsession with her is clearly genuine.

Alec is the antithesis of Tess, the child of nature and history. Alec is un-natural: he is identified with the modern, artifical settings of The Slopes and Sandbourne; he is out of place in his various borrowed rôles; he conspicuously adopts costumes and disguises. He is a modern man, a 'false' d'Urberville, son of a new-rich merchant class. Only in his desire is he allied with nature: a distortion of Tess's instinctive sensuality.

Although Alec and Angel appear alternately in the narrative (and never meet), they are constantly recalled in each other's absence: linked yet opposed. Alec represents 'the cruelty of lust': Angel, 'the fragility of love'. Alec's passion is animalistic: Angel's, 'ethereal'. You might even see Alec as body and Angel as mind: two extreme aspects of a whole healthy personality. Alec's chauvinism lies in dominating, Angel's in idealising, women — and both damage Tess. The parallels in detail between the men — their driving, 'conversions', costumes and so on – keep the triangle alive.

## Angel Clare

Angel

Angel balances Alec, illustrating the moral inadequacy of intellect without experience. Yet, despite his long absences, Hardy makes Angel interesting as a person torn by conflict, whom we can see developing during the novel.

Son of a clergyman, Angel has rejected religion, and refused the university education given to his brothers. Deep down, he feels deprived of his destiny. He compensates with a pride in his own 'intellectual freedom' and enlightenment, which actually makes him detached and intellectually inflexible. His ambition thwarted, he cultivates an indifference to social standards, and turns to farming.

Angel sometimes seems 'an intelligence rather than... a man'. At the club dance, he seems a 'tentative student of something and everything'. We rediscover him, still the detached observer–student, at Talbothays. There is something 'educated, reserved... differing' about him. He considers himself enlightened, and he defies social convention in marrying Tess. But his tendency to form a general impression by neglecting the details leads him to stereotype Tess as an ideal of unspoilt, virginal womanhood. His love for her is 'ethereal to a fault' — ominously inadequate in the face of the intensely physical Tess.

Too much thinking has hardened Angel: he lacks the generosity and spontaneity of Alec. He is insensitive to the feelings of others. For all his 'humanism', he lacks humanity. And beneath his liberal views, he is really very conventional. He prizes respectability (supposedly for his parents' sake) and adopts traditional male rôles in relation to Tess. As her instructor and protector, Angel is as dominating as Alec, in his own way.

The wedding night brings these tensions to the surface. When Angel realises that Tess is not the ideal woman he has been loving, he blames her, unable to take responsibility for, or look beyond, his own disillusionment. He is, after all, enslaved to 'custom and conventionality'. His intellectual inflexibility is revealed as emotional indequacy.

Yet Hardy allows Angel some sympathy. His tragedy is that years of detachment and philosophising have left him so unable to engage with real life that he 'hardly knew' he loved Tess until it was too late.

But he learns. In Brazil, suffering teaches him his own limitations, and Tess's true value. He comes home a changed man, and offers Tess a new humility, understanding and capacity for self-giving.

## The Durbeyfields

**John Durbeyfield** is physically and morally weak, a heart condition and a liking for drink adding to his laziness and irresponsibility. His newly-discovered ancestry feeds a vain pretension which allows him to abandon all attempts to provide for his struggling family. Too self-absorbed to be concerned for Tess, he even refuses to call the parson to her dying child, to hide the family's 'disgrace'. There is both humour and pathos in the gulf between his vanity and the hopeless degradation of his circumstances.

John's wife **Joan** is as irresponsible as a 'happy child'. She occasionally escapes 'the muck and muddle of rearing children' in music – and visits to the inn with her husband. She is both fatalistic (accepting her lot, John's defects and Tess's ruin) and opportunistic, seizing the chance offered by the rich Alec. Tess is saddened by the shallowness and self-interest of her mother's advice and reactions. Yet Joan shows flashes of conscience (at her irresponsibility towards Tess) and resilience in the face of hopeless drudgery. At the end, she admits that she has 'never really known' Tess.

John and Joan have given Tess a decayed heredity and a fresh beauty respectively, but they fail to give her the moral support that might have saved her. They allow the pressure of their irresponsibility to fall on her, setting in motion events that both lead her to Alec and make her vulnerable to his power. However, there is rich comedy and authentic detail in Hardy's portrayal of them, and their failings are firmly rooted in the social and economic conditions of their time.

## The Clares

The members of Angel's family portray different aspects of Hardy's view of religion. His brothers, **Felix** and **Cuthbert**, are stereotypes of narrow, self-satisfied, academic religion. We first see them rushing off to pursue their study of a theological treatise: Angel is already the non-conformist in staying to dance. Their later disapproval of his marriage, and the derogatory comments overheard by Tess at Emminster, suggest thoroughly pompous, superficial and un-Christian characters.

By contrast, **Mr and Mrs Clare** are presented as sincere, devout Christians. Though theologically dogmatic and socially conventional, they are redeemed by a touching unworldliness and a deep generosity of spirit. Angel recognises the heroic quality in his father's humble and selfless zeal (which, ironically, leads to Alec's conversion).

The Clares care deeply for Angel (the black sheep of their family), give self-sacrificingly to the needy, and are compassionate toward sinners. Indeed, Hardy suggests that Tess's inability to face them was her greatest misfortune, since their unworldly viewpoint would have made her 'a fairly choice sort of lost person for their love'.

## Rural characters

A range of minor 'rustics' appear and — in the confined setting of the narrative — reappear through the novel.

The **dairymaids** are distinct individuals. **Marian** is jolly, plump and pink-faced; **Retty Priddle**, from another once-great family, young, pretty, auburn-haired and sensitive; **Izz Huett** pale, dark-haired and passionate. Each comes to terms with loving and losing Angel in her own way: Marian in drink, Retty in attempted suicide and Izz in a near self-abandonment conquered by fairness to Tess. As dairymaids and field-women, they mirror Tess's experience ('the woman pays'), without the influence of her imagination, education or sexuality. By turns romantic, jealous, and affectionate, ultimately generous, they contribute to the warm impression of Talbothays. This lingers even to Flintcomb-Ash, where Marian and Izz support Tess, and finally appeal to Angel on her behalf.

**Dairyman Crick** and his wife are likewise at the heart of friendly Talbothays. Full of uncomplicated affection and rustic tales, Crick stands in stark opposition to the other male figures in Tess's life, most notably the chauvinistic, tyrannical and grudge-bearing farmer Groby. Crick unwittingly keeps touching the nerve of Tess's exaggerated sensitivity with his innocent, humorous tales, especially that of the seducer Jack Dollop. Mrs Crick, too, is an insightful commentator, spotting 'summat strange' in Angel and Tess on their brief return from Wellbridge.

Other characters – club-girls, drinkers and dancers, harvesters, migrating families – perform similar functions. They further the narrative: Car Darch, for example, forces Tess into Alec's treacherous 'protection'. They portray the erosion of rural life by social change. They share areas of Tess's experience, creating the sense of fellowship in an indifferent universe, yet emphasising her ultimate isolation. They form the kind of 'chorus' used in classical tragedy to give the ordinary person's view of events. They add a vein of humour which both relieves tension and heightens pathos. Yet a warmth and immediacy in the details of Hardy's portrayal brings them to life as characters in themselves.

# Themes and images in
## *Tess of the d'Urbervilles*

Nature

## Nature

*Tess of the d'Urbervilles* reflects Hardy's abiding love for a rural England in the throes of change. Nature, described in vivid detail, is not only a backdrop, but becomes part of Tess's story: she identifies with its moods and changes, reinforcing Hardy's own use of the 'pathetic fallacy' (the idea that nature is somehow in sympathy with human emotions) in the novel.

The rural community's work patterns and customs follow the **seasonal cycle**. Seasons are also used to intensify the imaginative impact of Tess's experience: autumnal ruin, summer courtship, mid-winter rejection, the false hopes of spring. They are ultimately indifferent to humanity, however: Tess's execution takes place in full summer.

**Landscape** also reflects Tess's experience: of falsehood (The Slopes), love (Talbothays) and despair (Flintcomb-Ash), although it too emphasises her insignificance at times. Images and episodes involving **animals** and **birds** emphasise Tess's instinctive nature. Her sexuality is suggested by comparison to 'a sunned cat', her innocence by the image of half-open flowers.

Nature contrasts with artificiality and 'progress'. Speed (as in Alec's driving) is threatening, and the threshing machine is a hellish vision set against the rhythm and companionship of harvest and dairy. The 'sylvan antiquity' of The Chase exposes the man-made shapes and colours of The Slopes. Even farming represents an attempt to control nature, though the field folk are generally seen in harmony with the land: Hardy mourns their move to towns as unnatural, like water forced to flow uphill.

Nature and natural qualities take on the force of moral values, by which people are judged: social convention is 'out of harmony' with nature, not Tess – despite her guilt.

Alec and Angel are both from 'unnatural' worlds, while Tess's instinctive responses of love and faith are truer than all their social conditioning and the 'conventional aspect' in herself which generates such misery.

**Society**

## Society

Hardy shows how 'accepted social law' and 'convention' are often unnatural and inhumane. He does this through the Durbeyfields' impoverished pretensions; the uncharitable snobbery of the Clare brothers; the tyrannical chauvinism of Alec and Groby; Angel's slavery to custom and convention. 'The woman pays', by a hypocritical double standard: Tess's cry that Angel's sexual transgression was 'just the same!' exposes a society that is unjust to women and quick to define 'sin', without looking beyond the action to the heart.

Conditions in rural England are portrayed with affection and honesty. Rural life can offer contentment, companionship – or extreme hardship. Talbothays reflects 'the happiest of all positions in the social scale', while Flintcomb-Ash epitomises the worst: harsh land, brutalising work and the exploitation of women's cheap labour. Hardy describes some of the changes of his day: the banishment to towns of those not directly employed on the land; the erosion of village life; loss of stability through the constant migration of farm labourers.

Despite the hardship and insecurity of working the land, Hardy foresees a greater alienation in technology: the grimy engine man is isolated and unaware, and the threshing machine a vision of horror. The railway symbolises the encroachment of material progress on a tranquil world.

Social changes are reflected in language: Tess speaks schooled English as well as local dialect, setting her apart from her community and placing her in a new world she does not fully understand. Costume is a similar motif, portraying the shallowness of social roles and of the modern man (such as Alec or Angel) whose identity is no longer rooted in the soil.

Consider how many critical events in the novel can be traced to social and economic pressures: Tess's vulnerability to Alec, for example, is sustained by them. Do you think Tess's whole story is an allegory of the careless destruction of peasant life by the forces of the modern age?

## Fate

**Fate**

The idea of fate – an inexorable power determining the course of events with total indifference to their human consequences – is an important theme in Hardy's novels. His characters are subject to forces beyond their control, typified by chance and coincidence. The cumulative effect of a series of random events suggests an underlying purpose or direction. This creates a sense that the future is pre-determined: the country folk are fatalistic and sensitive to omens and signs, and Tess feels that her life is doomed from the moment the horse is killed. Though she feels she deserves her ill-fortune, Hardy portrays fate as impersonal, morally indifferent and basically unfair.

Yet people still have to make choices and act on them, as if they were in control of their lives. The 'gods' (and the novelist) may already know and have determined the outcome, but the characters *experience* fate as a constant stream of events which they simply have to deal with, according to their background and personality. *Tess of the d'Urbervilles* is a great web of events linked to other events, inevitably or coincidentally. But Hardy stresses that his characters' responses to each event are part of that web: as he affirmed in *The Mayor of Casterbridge*, 'Character is Fate'. We may, for example, understand the outside forces that drive Tess back to Alec, but we recognise that with more courage or less pride, they may not have been so influential.

Hardy's vision is pessimistic: a 'blighted' world; the inevitability of death; the impersonal tyranny of chance. But he also affirms natural beauty, 'the inherent will to enjoy' and the essential value of human life, however brief and insignificant within the 'flux and reflux' of the universe. People can grow (like Angel), can rise above suffering and injustice (like Tess), and can find final fulfilment in death.

# Religion

Thomas Hardy experienced a loss of faith in his twenties, becoming an agnostic in an era of profound religious controversy (particularly over the role of science, in the wake of Charles Darwin's theory of evolution). He is sometimes called 'anti-Christian', but *Tess of the d'Urbervilles* reflects the complexity of his attitudes to religion.

Hardy's supreme values are tolerance and compassion. He bitterly attacks inflexible adherence to religious dogma for the inhumanity, hypocrisy and self-satisfaction that frequently accompany it. His portrayal of Angel's brothers and Mercy Chant is devastating in its exposure of self-righteous lack of charity. The parson who refuses to bury Tess's baby is totally morally inadequate: Hardy uses his most bitter humour on the gulf between the 'ecclesiastic' and the 'man'. The man with the paint pot symbolises judgemental doctrines out of harmony with nature. Alec's brief, shallow fanaticism is the ultimate, ironic portrayal of religion's failure to touch the heart.

Yet *Tess of the d'Urbervilles* is full of Biblical references. Though religious teachings feed Tess's guilt, at key moments a more profound natural faith uplifts her: strikingly, at the baptism of Sorrow. When she later echoes Angel's rather comfortless (and slightly pompous) beliefs, do you feel that his intellectual humanism is any 'better' than Tess's simple faith? Or that of Angel's father? Angel believes in 'the *spirit* of the Sermon on the Mount', but it is his father who practises it. Mr Clare is warmly portrayed as 'a man not merely religious, but devout': compassionate and sincere.

The past

# The past

The chronology of *Tess of the d'Urbervilles* is deceptively simple. Hardy conveys a constant awareness of the past within the present. Tess, Angel and Alec all try to escape the past, but, inevitably, it catches up with them.

**Ancestral past** is symbolised by the d'Urbervilles. The power of the old house is set against the degraded present of the Durbeyfields (mirroring Tess's own 'fall'). Past touches are present in heredity: Tess inherits facial features, pride, and perhaps even punishment (as they made others suffer) from the d'Urbervilles. The phantom coach, the sinister portraits at Wellbridge and the ominous burial vaults at Kingsbere have a powerful effect on Tess's life. As does Alec, the d'Urberville *without* a past.

**Personal past** has an obvious effect on Tess. Guilt makes her a prisoner of her past: her attempt to escape, or atone for, each crisis in her life leads her on to the next. Meanwhile, Angel's past has left him unfit to deal with the confession that might have broken history's hold on Tess. Alec's past (Tess herself) returns to find him, ending in his murder: ironically, the end of the 'new' d'Urberville line.

The **communal past** is seen in the rural people – their dialect and customs – and the antiquity of the land. Crick's tales and Joan's songs keep a continuity of tradition, while change is felt in deserted farms, migrations, the rise and fall of families. Tess's past catches up with her at Stonehenge, a piece of communal history 'older than the d'Urbervilles'.

Meanwhile, **omens** and **foreshadowings** complete the line that runs from past to future. At the end, inevitably, lies death, but also continuity: in the very last sentence, Angel and Liza-Lu arise and move on.

# ■ Text commentary

## Phase The First: The Maiden

## Chapter 1

*John Durbeyfield, a travelling dealer, is weaving his way home to the village of Marlott when he meets Parson Tringham, the antiquary. He learns that he is descended from the 'ancient and knightly' family of d'Urberville, now extinct. 'Sir John' is much taken with this idea and demands a carriage for his journey home.*

The title of the phase prepares us to meet Tess, the 'pure woman' of Hardy's

The past

subtitle, but we are kept in suspense. Hardy's decision to open the novel with this incident immediately identifies Tess's ancestry as a key element of the story. The theme of past and present is established. John's d'Urberville features are 'a little debased' – just as his name is corrupted and his circumstances 'declined' (to say the least). This is a continuous thread in the novel: later, we will see traces of the family features in Tess, the ruin of the true d'Urberville (Tess) by the false (Alec), and the scripture quoted by Parson Tringham – 'How are the mighty fallen' – on John's gravestone.

Note how the d'Urbervilles are linked with death. John dwells proudly on their vaults, coffins and skeletons at Kingsbere. His homeless family will take refuge there, later in the novel, with eventually fatal results.

> *Tess of the d'Urbervilles*, despite its tragic core, has a rich vein of comedy. Hardy often uses irony (sometimes bitterly), but his more affectionate style is seen here. John's attempt at aristocratic hauteur, flat on his back among the daisies, is frankly comic. Even so, his surprise that a band is there to greet him – funny though it is – strikes a darker note: he has forgotten Tess (as he will again) in his 'thoughts of greater things'. Do you think John is an immediately appealing character on first acquaintance?

## Chapter 2

*As John rides by in triumph, the girls of Marlott are celebrating May-time, his daughter Tess among them. Three strangers watch the dancing, and one – named Angel – joins in. As he is leaving he sees Tess looking after him, and wishes that he had danced with her.*

We are prepared for Tess's appearance – but again, kept in suspense – by an

extended description of the Vale of Blackmoor, which puts her firmly in a natural setting. The vale is 'fertile and sheltered', but its ways are 'tortuous' and 'miry': a foreshadowing of the way in which Tess's home later, and repeatedly, lets her down by its moral and economic confusion.

**Nature** Hardy also links the land to its history and customs, of which only traces remain. Note the legend of the 'beautiful white hart': even before we see Tess in white, it symbolises nature and innocence victimised by man.

## A young member of the band turned her head...

Finally, we meet Tess, in an intense passage of description. She is 'fine and

handsome'. Her 'mobile peony mouth and large innocent eyes' reflect the ambiguity of her appearance, combining childlike freshness with sexual potential. She stands out by the ribbon in her hair, which establishes a colour motif linking her with red and white: vividness and innocence – at this stage.

**Tess** Her reaction to teasing shows pride and perhaps over-sensitivity. She is a 'vessel of emotion untinctured by experience': innocent yet passionate.

## Among these on-lookers were three young men of a superior class...

We also see Angel for the first time, briefly. Hardy swiftly establishes his 'superior class', his unformed nature as a 'tentative student' of life, and the contrast to his religious brothers. He is also an 'on-looker': a hint of the detachment which affects his future relationship with Tess. Note that he

**Angel** fails to dance with her: the first 'abandonment'.

# Chapter 3

*Tess returns home and learns of her father's discovery. Her mother escapes briefly from the washing to 'find' her husband, who is out celebrating. When neither of them return, Tess goes in search of them.*

Hardy hints at qualities which will shape Tess's future: her sense of

responsibility for the family; the 'dreadful sting of remorse' which makes her so vulnerable to emotional blackmail; the sense (symbolised by language) that she is an outsider in a family that will consistently fail to understand her needs.

Joan Durbeyfield still has something of the freshness she has

**Tess** given Tess, but there is a gulf between her 'lumber of superstitions and folk-lore' and Tess's educated intelligence. Trapped in 'the muck and muddle of rearing children', Joan stays cheerful by ignoring chores as long as possible, and by 'seeking' her husband at the inn, where she is able to forget about her everyday life for a while and shut her eyes to John's defects of character. Who seems the more responsible adult to you here: Tess or her mother?

Meanwhile, the children are 'passengers' and 'captives', compelled to accept the hardships caused by their shiftless parents. Hardy stresses the irony of their lack of choices in a life they never asked for.

# Chapter 4

*At Rolliver's Inn, Joan plans to send Tess to claim kinship with rich Mrs d'Urberville, hoping to 'put her in the way of a grand marriage'. John is drunk, so Tess has to drive the beehives to market with her young brother Abraham. Dozing, they are hit by a speeding mail cart, and their horse Prince is killed. Tess, knowing his importance to the family, blames herself.*

For this first crisis in Tess's life, which leads to the next and greater one, Hardy carefully balances responsibility and chance.

Abraham's innocent prattling prefaces the disaster with a discussion about fate: he wonders what life would have been like if the world had been 'sound' instead of 'blighted'. (Tess has used the familiar image of apples, so this is not as inappropriate as it sounds.) Tess, daydreaming about her mother's plans, dozes off. This makes her take full responsibility for the accident,

**Fate**

with 'no excuse' – but Hardy has suggested a number of contributing factors: John's drunkenness, Tess's lack of sleep, the mail cart's speed, bad luck. Would *you* blame Tess for what happened?

There are foreshadowings of the future. Sir John's haughty refusal to sell his 'charger' to the knacker highlights Tess's concern about their livelihood, while at Rolliver's, we saw Joan deliberately planning to exploit her daughter's looks to attract 'some noble gentleman': both features of her future relationship with Alec. Tess is splashed with 'crimson drops' from Prince's wound: the red of her ribbon has become blood, and pure white the pallor of

**Tess**

shock. When she seems to see herself 'in the light of a murderess', we sense more than her self-conscious guilt feelings: this will, eventually, be the end of the road on which Tess has just embarked.

# Chapter 5

*The trading business collapses and Tess, feeling responsible, is persuaded to visit Mrs d'Urberville. At The Slopes she meets Alec Stoke-d'Urberville, whose family has merely adopted the old name. Alec, forceful and sensual, turns an arrogant charm on a confused Tess.*

Guilt overcomes Tess's pride, and sends her to The Slopes. We are helped to understand her sense of responsibility by a review of how she came to take on 'the family burdens', her mother being just 'a happy child' herself (prefiguring Tess as the true child-mother, later).

## She alighted from the van at Trantridge Cross...

The impoverishment of the Durbeyfields is contrasted sharply with the new-

rich merchant family who have, out of snobbery, taken their name. The Slopes, with its glass-houses and modern (red) brick buildings, is artificial against the backdrop of the 'truly venerable' Chase. Alec's world is alien to nature and the past, and therefore to Tess herself.

**Society**

When Alec appears for the first time, it is as the caricature of a melodramatic villain, with his curling moustaches and 'bold rolling eye'. He uses fluent charm, flattering Tess and calling her 'Coz' (cousin), with a chauvinistic force that emphasises her vulnerability. His pressing strawberries and roses on her shows a forceful sensuality and generosity by which Tess is understandably confused: she is 'half-pleased,

**Alec**

half-reluctant'. Note that the fruit and flowers (both red) have been ripened unseasonably early: a symbol of the 'fulness of growth' in Tess which makes her appear 'more of a woman than she really was'. It is this luxuriant quality that attracts Alec.

---

Alec's colours have been immediately identified: red, linking him to Tess in sensuality and violence, and black (to her white), emphasising the gulf between them in purity of heart. What is the effect of calling Alec 'the blood-red ray in the spectrum of her young life'?

---

### Thus the thing began

Hardy steps back from the action to point out the fateful importance of the

event. Tess is 'doomed' to attract Alec, instead of the 'right' man who is 'waiting in crass obtuseness till the late time came'. Do you sense who the obtuse latecomer might be? Hardy, as omniscient narrator, sees a line between present and future that is hidden from his characters. Do you find his comments

**Fate**

intrusive or helpful?

# Chapter 6

*Arriving home, Tess finds a letter – purporting to be from Mrs d'Urberville – asking her to look after the fowl-farm at The Slopes. After failing to find work elsewhere, Tess reluctantly agrees.*

Hardy builds up tension by hinting that Tess is being lured into danger. She has pricked herself on one of Alec's roses: an 'ill omen'. Joan recognises the offer of work as an artful way of getting her daughter to The Slopes, but ascribes it to *Mrs* d'Urberville, whose handwriting seems 'rather masculine'...

Tess agrees to go only because she feels financially responsible for the family, and can find no work elsewhere: a pattern which repeats itself later, forcing her to go to Flintcomb-Ash. Note how her guilt makes her sensitive to the children's tears, her father's cough, her mother's exaggerated labours.

Tess

## Chapter 7

*Joan dresses Tess in her best clothes, and the family see her on her way.*

Hardy emphasises her parents' role in Tess's ruin, although he suggests that

her submission and pride allow it (now, as later). Joan dresses her deliberately to encourage Alec, and later is complacent about the likelihood of Tess's being seduced: Alec will marry her 'after'. Both parents are as opportunistically prepared to auction their empty title as they are their daughter. The

Fate

children's tears and Joan's misgivings, on Tess's departure, heighten the sense that she has been sacrificed. Joan calls Tess's face her 'trump card', while John thinks of her d'Urberville blood: both inheritances are leading Tess to Alec, and ruin.

Alec is in costume as the 'handsome, horsey young buck': the first of many disguises in which he appears. We also note that Tess is wearing the white dress from the club-walking: we see her, at the moment Alec claims her, just as the departing Angel saw her – a distant white shape. This link between the men sets up the fateful triangle.

## Chapter 8

*Alec frightens Tess with his reckless driving, tricking her into holding on to him, and finally demanding a kiss in return for slowing down. Tess's distaste angers him, and she has to resort to trickery of her own – letting her hat fly off – to stop the carriage, and walk the rest of the way.*

This is the first of many duels between Alec and Tess. She is defiant and spirited,

despite her physical vulnerability. (Tess's strong independence of Alec, for all his apparent dominance, is balanced in the novel by her utter dependence on Angel, for all his apparent consideration.) Note that again Tess's pride and sense of guilt (Alec's speed reminds her of the accident to the horse) forces her through a moment when she might have turned back.

Tess

**'Now, damn it – I'll break both our necks!'**

Alec is still the model of villainy: reckless driving, curses, 'inexorable' demands. Do you find his behaviour realistic, or even excusable? He is 'capriciously passionate': carried away. He relates to Tess as his social conditioning has taught him to, on the chauvinistic assumption that women exist to be 'mastered' (like horses). He believes that country girls have casual morals

Alec

(borne out, as we later find, by his experience). Remember that Tess's appearance belies her innocence. Alec is also proud: he is genuinely put out when she wipes off his kiss. But his temper swiftly clears: he shows emotional honesty, spontaneity and even 'a sort of fierce distress'.

# Chapter 9

*Tess looks after the fowls at The Slopes for the blind Mrs d'Urberville, and (taught by Alec) whistles to the old lady's pet bullfinches. Alec behaves himself, with careful charm, and Tess begins to feel secure in his presence.*

The episode opens with a farm cottage 'overrun with ivy' and given over to

birds, reflecting Hardy's theme of the passing of rural life.

The domestication of the birds, however benign, is a reflection of the dangerous stability of Tess's new relations with Alec: mastery disguised by civility. His behaviour makes her feel 'quite safe'. She is disarmed by his teaching her to whistle (despite its sensual aspects) and by his 'playful dialogue'.

Society

Yet we sense a subtle threat: Alec's familiarity is a deliberate ploy to make Tess 'pliable under his hands'. He is secretly watching her. The chapter ends with an ironic false security, as she dismisses any fear of 'ambush'.

# Chapter 10

*Tess visits Chaseborough on a Saturday night. She is reluctant to join the rowdy dance but, refusing Alec's escort, she waits to return with the drunken Trantridge group. Innocently laughing at an accident to one of the other girls, Car Darch, Tess finds herself in a fight. Alec appears to 'rescue' her.*

The 'coincidence' of market and fair creates a wild, reckless setting in which Tess is isolated and uneasy. The dance scene carries heavy undertones of passion: a haze of dust, warmth, perspiration, loss of control and Hardy's allusions to mythological rapes and sexual pursuits. Ironically, Tess fears to leave alone because of 'roving characters of possibly ill intent': we know Alec is hovering outside. Note his faintly devilish appearance, laughing in the red glow of his cigar.

Car Darch ('Queen of Spades', an ominous note) is dark, violent and 'careless': she and her sister have both been Alec's lovers. Yet, glowing with alcohol and moolight, she and her fellows seem joyously one with nature.

Fate

This vivid scene highlights Tess's vulnerability and creates the extreme circumstances required to force her into Alec's arms: we really feel that 'at almost any other moment of her life she would have refused'. Note that, under pressure, Tess 'abandoned herself to her impulse' to go with Alec: a reckless submission we shall see again.

# Chapter 11

*Riding alone in the dark, Alec woos Tess, telling her that her suspicions of him are unjust and that he has given her family gifts. Tess, confused by gratitude and sleepiness, does not completely reject him. Lost in the foggy Chase, Alec leaves Tess to seek a landmark, and returns to find her asleep...*

Various factors lull Tess into passivity: she is 'inexpressably weary'; a 'faint

Tess

luminous fog' surrounds them; Alec has given not just the longed-for horse, but also toys for the children. He finds her sleeping – as she was at the death of the horse. Hardy dwells, with a kind of helplessness, on intimate details: the warmth of her breath, tears on her lashes, white muslin against dead leaves. He also describes the utter serenity of The Chase, with its 'gentle roosting birds' and ancient trees.

> Would you call Alec's act 'rape'? It is not described: the narrator is 'absent' – as he is for the birth of Tess's baby, her confession, her murder of Alec, her execution. Why do we not witness these events? Hardy has to suggest what happens with great delicacy (so as not to offend his original readers) but also to present Tess as wronged, innocent, still a 'pure woman'. Do you sense a quiet outrage on Tess's behalf?

## Darkness and silence ruled everywhere...

You may find this section intrusive, but it poses some hard questions. Hardy

Fate

invites us to find a 'sense of order' in what has happened. Where was God? Where was justice? Can we simply say that Tess's ancestors treated others this way, so now it is her turn? The only answer Hardy can suggest is that there *is* no sense or purpose to her fate: 'It was to be'. Fate is basically *unfair*: how does this affect our sense of Tess's essential goodness and purity?

> Classical tragedy shows the downfall of a basically good person through fate, aided by a flaw in his own character, in order to arouse the audience's pity and

terror at the human condition. Hardy wrote: 'The best tragedy... is that of the *worthy* encompassed by the *inevitable*'. If the hero deserves his suffering, we will not pity him; if it is unnecessary, we will not be awed by his brave struggles; if it is completely inevitable, we will simply feel desperate – hence the flawed hero with whom we can identify and for whom we can hope. Do you think Hardy intended *Tess of the d'Urbervilles* to be a tragedy?

The phase ends where it began, with Tess's hereditary past and community past. The personal past, however, has just changed the whole of the rest of her life.

# Phase The Second: Maiden No More

## Chapter 12

*Some weeks later, Tess has left Alec and is returning home, proudly rejecting his offers of money and reconciliation. She meets a man painting Biblical texts which shame her. Back in Marlott, Joan is selfishly vexed that Tess has not got Alec to marry her.*

The second phase opens, like the first, with a figure returning on foot to Marlott – but that was spring, and this is autumn: the phase title is explicit about what has happened to Tess. Alec arrives in the carriage, and the parallels with their previous drive ('in the opposite direction along the same road') emphasise the change in Tess's life.

Tess was 'dazed' by Alec for a while, but never sincerely loved him. Despite her self-loathing for her own 'weakness', she shows a flash of proud spirit in refusing him and his money: foreshadowing her later resistance. Alec is chauvinistically cynical about Tess's hurt innocence ('That's what every woman says'), but he is also aware of his own villainy. He seems genuine in his offer to 'pay' for wronging Tess, and is affectionate towards her – without, now, having anything to gain by it.

Alec

### Tess did not look after him...

You may find the man with the paint pot contrived, but he is merely meant

to be a symbol of the 'unnaturalness' of judgemental religion and Tess's guilt feelings. His red paint (note the colour) is a 'hideous defacement' of the landscape, and the words he writes, about damnation and (implied) adultery, are 'grotesque': Tess instinctively feels that God would not say such things. The man himself is helpful and cheerful (if ghoulish in his enthusiasm), but Hardy emphasises his functional role with a final coincidence: the mention of a Mr Clare (whom we meet later, as Angel's father).

Religion

**'Well! – my dear Tess!'**

This is the first of Tess's returns home in distress to find no support or comfort. Self-centred and hypocritical, Joan is vexed at Tess's failure to 'get' Alec to marry her. Tess, by contrast, has not even considered the possibility of such a 'social salvation'. For the first time (though not the last) she is belatedly stung into sharing the blame: 'Why didn't you tell me there was danger in menfolk?' she reproaches her mother.

## Chapter 13

*Despite the half-envious interest of the other girls, Tess is depressed. She goes to church, but the whispers drive her away, and she retreats to her room, only going out at night for lonely walks in the hills.*

We glimpse society's attitude to Tess's 'ruin'. The village girls, who love her,

**Society**

tease her good-humouredly and are half-envious of her glamorous experience. In church, the looks and whispers are of a different kind: this section of the community later turns the Durbeyfields out, because Tess is not a 'proper woman'. Hardy links social bigotry with religious hypocrisy: note the pretended prayers.

**Nature**

From society, we turn to nature. Tess, walking the hills, is 'an integral part of the scene'. Yet she projects her self-condemnation onto nature, and feels alienated from it, 'a figure of Guilt intruding into the haunts of Innocence'. Hardy says these 'moral hobgoblins' come from Tess's own mind and the conventions she has learned: they are 'out of harmony with the actual world', not she. Does this view make you more or less sympathetic to Tess?

## Chapter 14

*The following summer, Tess is working with the harvesters, having had a baby. She is recovering her spirits – but the baby falls ill. Her father refuses to shame the family by calling the parson, so Tess baptises the child herself, naming him Sorrow. He dies and, refused a Christian burial by the parson, is buried by Tess.*

As in our first sight of Tess, Hardy first gives a general description of the scene

**Tess**

and people before the eye is drawn to one figure, finally identified as Tess: an intensely visual technique. The scene prepares us to find Tess re-emerging to familiar surroundings, natural work and friendly companions. The scene where she suckles her baby is touching and encouraging, the fieldfolk roughly sympathetic. Hardy builds our hopes with an account of how Tess has recovered her spirits, but just as she is 'almost gay', fate intervenes again.

## 'O merciful God, have pity...'

After conventionally lurid images of hell (relayed with bitter irony), Tess's  simple faith transcends orthodoxy with a 'transfiguring effect': the 'girl–mother' of 'immaculate beauty' (echoes of the Virgin Mary) glows as she baptises her dying infant, surrounded by awed children. In contrast to this 'ecstasy of faith', we meet the parson, struggling to deny his scepticism. Hardy ironically shows the 'man' in conflict with the 'ecclesiastic', attacking the Church's adherence to dogma instead of humanity, to 'strict notions' instead of 'noble impulses'.

**Religion**

# Chapter 15

*For over a year, Tess works at home, muses over her past and future, and begins to hope that she can escape the past in new surroundings. As spring comes round again, she is offered work at Talbothays.*

As anniversaries pass, Tess looks back over her past, and realises that time also leads forward to death. This changes her from a simple girl to a complex woman: matured, not cast down, by her 'turbulent experience'. Marlott has nearly forgotten the past — but Tess's 'keen consciousness' of humiliation makes her want to escape both. As spring returns, she is moved, like a wild animal, by the stirring of new life. See how Hardy links Tess and nature in this surging sense of hope and rebirth. What do you anticipate from the title of the next phase: 'The Rally'?

---

**Hardy's style**

You should already have some sense of Hardy's style. Think as you read what you find effective and ineffective: here are some areas to consider.

Hardy's style is sometimes criticised for the following features:

- Complex, clumsy sentences and long, unfamiliar words
- Use of allusions (references to literature, mythology, the Bible)
- Intrusion of the narrator to comment on the action
- Use of imagery, symbolism, omens and cross-references to hammer home the significance of events
- Extensive use of coincidence
- Stereotyping characters to reinforce their functional roles

In what way are these features weaknesses? How might they also be strengths? Would you defend Hardy against any of these criticisms?

---

### Dialogue

Hardy's rustic dialect is much admired for its realistic tone, ramblings, implied accents and dialect expressions. Look at the Durbeyfields (and, later, Dairyman Crick). Otherwise, you may find speech varying from convincingly natural, to emotionally overwrought, to stiltedly literary. Think what is appropriate to a speaker's education, intelligence and psychological state.

### Description

Hardy's visual (and symbolic) details have great impact. The narrator/observer is fascinated with Tess, and the natural descriptions are both realistic and full of mood and significance. Choose your favourite passages for study.

### Narrative

The viewpoint varies. Events are told through the eyes of:

- *The omniscient narrator.* Check your response to the end of Chapters 5 and 11. The point of view can be subtle: look at the end of Chapter14.

- *Witnesses.* Hardy occasionally suggests that he is relaying a true story, told to him by people who saw the events or knew Tess.

- *The main characters.* A more involved, subjective view. We often join Angel watching Tess, or Tess observing natural scenes. Beware of Hardy expressing his *own* views through them, in a conspicuous or unnatural way.

- *Minor characters.* Suspense is created by the observation of Alec's approach in Chapter 46, and the (implied) murder of Alec (Chapter 56).

# Self-test (Questions) Phases One & Two

(Numbers in brackets refer to the chapters in whch the answers can be found.)

**Uncover the plot**

Delete two of the three alternatives given, to find the correct plot. Beware possible misconceptions and muddles.

In June/May/February, in the Vale of Froom/Marlott/Blackmoor, John Durbeyfield (a poacher/farmer/dealer) discovers he is a d'Urbeville/Durberville/ d'Urberville. Tess is urged to go to Wintoncester/Chaseborough/Trantridge to claim kinship with Alec/Mrs/Sir John d'Urberville, and when Abraham/Tib/Prince is killed she agrees. At The Slopes/The Chase/The Fair, she meets Alec/Angel/ Jack, who offers her work as a dairymaid/fowl-keeper/harvester. After a dance at Marlott/Trantridge/Chaseborough, Tess gets into a fight with the Queen of Spades/Hearts/Diamonds: Alec 'rescues' her but in the foggy/rainy/bright May/ September/January night, seduces her. She returns home carrying his roses/child/ gifts. Tess recovers her money/health/spirits, but then John/Sorrow/Abraham dies. Some time later, Tess resolves to leave/marry/die.

### Who? What? Why? When? Where? How?

1 Who represents 'religion' in these phases, and what effect do they have on Tess?
2 Who are the three young onlookers at the club-walking, by name?
3 What does Alec give Tess on their first meeting? What does he give her family?
4 What reasons are suggested for Tess's recovering her spirits (14)?
5 What factors contribute to the accident to the horse?
6 When does Tess get the letter inviting her to Talbothays?
7 Why does Tess finally consent to take work at The Slopes?
8 Why will the parson not give Sorrow a Christian burial?
9 How does Joan Durbeyfield contribute to Tess's ruin?
10 How does Tess sum up her feelings for Alec?

### Who is this?

From your knowledge of the characters in the novel, identify the following people:

1 Who is 'simply an additional one, and that not the eldest, to her own long family'?
2 Who says: 'You should read my hottest ones... They'd make ye wriggle'?
3 Who is 'a mere vessel of emotion untinctured by experience'?
4 Who has 'more conceit than energy or health'?
5 Who has 'touches of barbarism in his contours'?
6 Who is a 'desultory tentative student of something and everything'?

### Looking ahead

What future events do the following incidents foreshadow?

1 Angel fails to dance with Tess, and leaves, dismissing her from his mind (2)
2 At Prince's burial, Tess looks like 'she regarded herself in the light of a murderess' (4)
3 Tess is sleeping when Prince is killed (4)
4 Alec forces early strawberries and roses on Tess (5)
5 The man with the paint pot recommends a visit to Mr Clare of Emminster (12)

### Ironic, isn't it?

What is ironic about the following lines, given what you know about the novel?

1 John sees Tess off to Trantridge with the words: 'Goodbye, my maid' (7)
2 Tess fears to leave Chaseborough alone because of 'roving characters of possibly ill intent' outside (10)
3 Joan reproaches Tess for her ruin: 'Why didn't ye think of doing some good for your family, instead o' thinking only of yourself?' (12)
4 Alec says: 'I was born bad, and I have lived bad, and I will die bad in all probability' (12)
5 Tess, leaving Marlott, resolves that 'there should be no more d'Urberville air castles' (16)

### Pointers

At the end of which incidents does Hardy tell us:

1 'Thus the thing began'?
2 ' "It was to be". There lay the pity of it'?

# Phase The Third: The Rally

## Chapter 16

*Tess walks through spring countryside to the fertile, expansive Vale of Froom, the beauty of which lifts her spirits. 'In good heart, and full of zest for life', she follows the cows home at milking-time to Talbothays.*

The phase opens with another journey, again in the 'opposite direction'. Its

**Nature**

title suggests a new and brighter period of Tess's life, and this chapter strongly establishes the note of hope.

After the 'silent, reconstructive years' Tess is finally mastered by 'the irresistable, universal, automatic tendency to find sweet pleasure somewhere'. Her hopes are reflected in the Valley of the Great Dairies, which is fertile, expansive and cheering. There is a 'change in the quality of the air from heavy to light', and the Froom is as 'clear as the pure River of Life'. Though Tess is an insignificant figure against the wide expanse of the valley ('like a fly on a billiard table'), she is in tune with it.

**Religion**

Tess's natural faith finds expression again, in a joyous, instinctive hymn of praise.

## Chapter 17

*Tess joins the milking. A dairyman is asked to play the harp: he stands out as a gentleman, despite his milking clothes, and Tess recognises him as the young man who joined in the May-time dancing in Marlott. That night in the dairyhouse, she overhears whispers about a Mr Angel Clare.*

Tess immediately fits in at Talbothays. The work is quiet, rythmic, serene.

**Angel**

To encourage the cows, a harp is called for – but we are left in suspense through a funny tale before we learn who the harper is. His speech is immediately different from the others' rich dialect. Tess/Hardy identifies something 'educated, reserved, subtle, sad, differing' about him: he is still trying to find his rôle in life, and is already 'more thoughtful' than the

stranger who impulsively joined in the dance. The whispering dairymaids remind us of Angel's name and his harp. Do you feel that 'angel' is an appropriate role for him? Is Hardy being ironic? Or establishing the ideal in Tess's mind? Or is he stressing Angel's 'spiritual' nature, to balance Alec's fleshly one?

The past

Tess feels she has made a fresh start, but there is lots of history at Talbothays. Angel is a man from Tess's innocent past – but note the echoes of her guilty one in the emphasis on Angel's costume, and the identification of Mr Clare of Emminster (mentioned by the man with the paint pot) as Angel's father.

# Chapter 18

*Hardy fills in Angel's background: his rejection of his family's faith, forfeiting of a university education, years in 'desultory studies' and decision to try farming. One day, Angel notices Tess and, feeling that he has seen her somewhere before, starts to take an interest in her.*

Angel

Angel's history has five important aspects: (a) His loss of faith (to an extent reflecting Hardy's own). Through this, Angel forfeits his hopes of a university education, for which he proceeds to compensate. (b) The resulting 'indifference to social forms and observances', which enables him to marry Tess – but cannot cope with her confession. (c) His turning to country life and people, and discovery of nature. (d) His tendency to intellectualise everything, and particularly to generalise. Note how swiftly he stereotypes Tess as a 'fresh and virginal daughter of Nature'. (e) His brief affair.

Fate

Consider the chain of apparently random events that have brought both Angel and Tess to Talbothays at the same time. The coincidence of their previous meeting is also highlighted, as arousing Angel's interest. Note that at the moment Angel notices Tess, Dairyman Crick's knife and fork look 'like the beginning of a gallows'. What effect does this have?

# Chapter 19

*Tess, walking in the garden, is captivated by the sound of Angel's harp: caught dreaming, she shows an imagination that intrigues him. Little by little they learn more of each other. Wishing to impress him, Tess plans to tell Angel about her ancestry, but Crick tells her that Angel hates old families.*

Nature

The relationship of Tess and Angel is reflected in nature: a serene summer evening. The images created by the wild garden hover between passion ('mists of pollen' recalling the night of Tess's seduction) and degradation (slug-slime, blights, stains). Look at this first conversation between the two: do you find its strange intensity effective, or unlikely? Angel is surprised by Tess's tragic view of life, while Tess wonders why so 'bookish' a man should choose to be a farmer. Neither has the clue to the other's secret – Tess's seduction, Angel's disappointed ambition. They grow in intimacy 'without attempting to pry into each other's history'. Revelation, as we know, will come later – and too late.

Tess worships Angel for his superior intellect, but she is surely right to feel that books cannot teach her the answers to life. What does it say about Angel that he has 'casually mentioned something to her about pastoral life in ancient Greece'?

**The past**

Tess hopes to win Angel's respect with her d'Urberville ancestry. In fact, it comes to symbolise his misconceptions about her. He will be falsely impressed with its social value and falsely repelled by its symbolic decadence, before realising its real value: its emotional and imaginative appeal.

## Chapter 20

*As the summer ripens, Tess and Angel are thrown together in morning tasks and walks, 'balanced on the edge of a passion'.*

This is a short, incredibly intense chapter, worth reading closely. Talbothays

**Nature**

is described as an idyllic pastoral world in which Angel and Tess discover each other amid the fullness of nature: pulled together by its 'irresistible law'. This is the peak of Tess's happiness. However, note the mix of light and dark; the fog, the mist on Tess's eyelashes (as on the night of her seduction); Biblical allusions to fallen women set against Angel's dangerous fantasies of ideal womanhood. We are brought down to earth by solid Dairyman Crick.

## Chapter 21

*The butter is not forming – by rural lore, a sign that somebody is in love. Tess, upset by a tale of the seducer Jack Dollop, goes outside and the butter immediately forms. That night, she hears Marian, Retty and Izz confess their love for Angel, sighing that he will never marry a farm girl. Tess muses that a farm girl would be a perfect wife, and that she could win Angel, but feels that she can never let any man marry her.*

Just as the butter points to love between Tess and Angel, the amusing tale of Jack Dollop (forced to marry the girl he has seduced) brings back, in a rush, all Tess's self-conscious guilt. Morbidly sensitive, she is upset by Crick's innocently calling her 'maidy' and by her awareness that everyone else thought the story was funny. (It was: Hardy tells such tales well.)

Marian, Retty and Izz put Tess's suffering in context. They are distinct individuals in their looks and temperament, and natural in their speech and

Tess

sentiments: romantic, shy, jealous and defiant by turns. But they are also, as a group, contrasted with Tess. Their simple, frankly-expressed feelings emphasise how all her superior qualities (passion, education, sexuality) conspire to over-complicate her life. Tess knows she has the power to attract Angel — but is too self-conscious to seize the chance.

# Chapter 22

*Now there is a sharp taste in the butter, caused by garlic in the grass: everyone turns out to search for it. Tess self-sacrificingly draws Angel's attention to the other girls, and thereafter tries to avoid him.*

The search for the garlic is another portrait of the natural companionship and rhythms of fieldwork, heightening the tension of Angel and Tess's acute physical awareness of each other. Tess has 'moodily' decided that Izz or Retty would make a better wife for Angel, and that she should give them every chance. Note the affectionate irony with which Hardy describes her self-sacrificing mood, and her assumption that Angel's coolness to the other dairymaids is due to a sense of duty — rather than just lack of sensitivity. Tess is right, though, that Angel 'had the honour of all the dairymaids in his keeping': they all suffer at his indifference, and he almost compromises Izz's honour in Chapter 40.

# Chapter 23

*Tess goes out to church with the other girls, but the lane is flooded. Angel appears and offers to carry them all across, holding Tess with controlled passion. The other girls recognise his preference for Tess and Tess confesses to herself that she loves him. That night, the suffering girls tell Tess that Angel's family has chosen a wife for him. Tess gives up hope.*

Again, the dairymaids are individual in their response to being carried, yet

Tess

Society

one in their hopeless passion. They are generous and fatalistic about Angel's favouring Tess, 'confiding and warm' when she renounces him, dignified in hopeless resignation. We have already seen the more complex sensitivities of Tess: her acute awareness of Angel's nearness, the conflict between hope and self-denial. In her 'hungry heart', she has admitted that she loves him. Think of how her past experience of 'love' might intensify her attraction to Angel — gallant, tender, but self-controlled — at this point.

Hardy shows sympathy for the three women oppressed by passion, 'an emotion thrust on them by cruel Nature's law'. Note, however, that their feelings of hopelessness and futility are rooted only in 'the eye of civilisation': their social class forbids all hope of marriage to such a man. This allows them to be resigned to their lot. For Tess, however, 'the eyes of propriety' have a more painful meaning, to do with personal worth rather than social position.

## Chapter 24

*At the height of summer, Tess and Angel are in the fields. Watching her, his passion is quickened and impulsively he embraces her. As Tess cries and withdraws, he tells her he loves her. A corner has been turned.*

Nature again mirrors the relationship between Tess and Angel. The oppressive  heat and maddening gadflies of summer reflect the pressure of Angel's passion. Hardy continues to let the tension build slowly: Angel focuses on every sensual detail of Tess's features until he is overcome by excitement and – leaving aside all caution – embraces her. With equally unreflecting 'inevitableness', she yields.

**Nature**

Do you find this a satisfying climax? Angel thinks that he finds 'nothing ethereal' in Tess's face, but a 'real incarnation' whose imperfections he loves. *Has* he yet seen and accepted the real, physical Tess? He holds himself back from kissing her: do you think he has the capacity for passion that she does? Tess feels happy for a moment, but then grows tearful and agitated: Alec still remains between them, as Angel's very respectfulness reminds us.

Angel and Tess are in the grip of a 'stubborn and resistless tendency'. Are you inclined to be hopeful about 'The Consequence'?

## Phase The Fourth: The Consequence

## Chapter 25

*Angel reflects on his feelings for Tess, and decides to seek advice. At Emminster, he avoids Mercy (the girl his parents wish him to marry) and feels like a foreigner in his parents' home. After Talbothays, his brothers seem narrow-minded and his parents somewhat puritanical.*

Angel is shocked by the 'unpremeditation' of his passion: ironically, since he goes on to plan and analyse it here. His concern not to ruin Tess's 'single opportunity of existence' shows how different he is to the thoughtless Alec – but is it possible to think too much? Note that he has hoped to 'calmly view' life from the 'screened alcove' of Talbothays.

**Angel**

## Clare knew her well...

Emminster epitomises the religious values to which Angel will revert in crisis.

Mercy Chant is quickly sketched as a prim figure opposed to the 'impassioned, summer-steeped heathens' at Talbothays. The Reverends Felix and Cuthbert are introduced as young men 'correct to their remotest fibre', slaves to social custom and limited in outlook: one 'all Church', the other 'all College'. They deplore Angel's social deterioration: later,

**Religion**

their casual disapproval is a cruel blow to Tess. Mr Clare, however, stands out: an 'earnest, God-fearing man', he is also sincere, kind-hearted and unselfish.

> The general atmosphere at Emminster is austere and rather stuffy. All the talk and description is formal and about doctrines, books, customs, duties. Angel feels 'foreign' here after the natural country life at Talbothays. He prides himself on a wider perspective and knowledge of life than his university-educated brothers: ironically, he later reveals a narrow-mindedness very like theirs.

# Chapter 26

*Angel sounds his parents out about marriage. While praising Mercy Chant, they are cautiously open-minded about Angel's choice, as long as she is orthodox in her faith. As Angel is leaving, his father mentions that he tried, unsuccessfully, to convert a young delinquent called d'Urberville.*

The irony of Angel's supposed enlightenment deepens. He believes he is condescending to his parents' middle-class prejudices by presenting Tess as a 'good Christian girl': he loves Tess for 'her soul, her heart, her substance', without the 'varnish of conventionality'. Yet he describes her in terms which show both his own conventionality and his false view of Tess.

**Angel**

Among the adjectives he rightly applies to her – 'honest-hearted, receptive, intelligent' – is 'chaste as a vestal' (virgin).

As Angel returns to Talbothays to propose to Tess, we see shadows of her

past, in the 'ghostly legend' of the d'Urberville coach (a recurring motif) and in Mr Clare's meeting with Alec. This incident shows the 'hero under the pietist' in Mr Clare. It also resonates with irony: Angel is unaware of the link between himself and Alec. The Clares' pious hopes for the sinner prefigure his return as 'The Convert'. Do you think these effects justify Hardy's use of an unlikely coincidence?

**The past**

# Chapter 27

*Angel returns to Tess. While they are skimming the milk, he asks her to marry him. Tess refuses, though she does confess her love for him: he assumes he has been too sudden. Changing the subject, he tells her about his father and Alec: Tess is even more determined to renounce him.*

The contrast between Talbothays and Emminster is accentuated by the

Tess

richness of nature. Tess, just woken from a nap, is compared to a snake and to a 'sunned cat': langorous, sensual images. Contrast the vivid style of this description with that of Angel's proposal and Tess's 'careworn', conscientious refusal. How do you regard Tess's belief that she ought not to marry anyone, after what she has done? Put yourself in Angel's place. What would you think of her response?

Note that Tess is, for the first time, 'driven to subterfuge': not just reticence, but deception. Hardy rather pointedly makes Angel the one to mention Alec: this keeps pressure on Tess's (and the reader's) awareness of her secret.

# Chapter 28

*Tess continues to resist Angel's proposals, finally agreeing to explain on Sunday. She realises, with fear and excitement, that she is going to accept him. But Saturday night arrives and she is still torn...*

Tess smothers her feelings, and continues to avoid a decision. Angel can only assume that her refusal to marry him is due to a sense of social inferiority. In fact, she fears to cause him regret for his 'blindness' in marrying her, once her secret is discovered. (If this seems unlikely, remember that it is exactly what does happen.)

Tess is a 'sheaf of susceptibilities' – both pleasure and pain. The clear

Nature

admission of her desire highlights Angel's patronising view of her as an innocent virgin: his own brand of chauvinism. Note his joke about her being about as experienced as a wild flower opening itself for the first time. By contrast, Tess escapes to a thicket of pollard willows, 'tortured out of their natural shape' as Tess is by her conscience. Nature is *not* chaste. It sides with desire against 'scrupulousness': here it even seems 'monstrous' to the tormented Tess.

# Chapter 29

*It is Sunday. Dairyman Crick has fresh news of the seducer Jack Dollop who has been trapped into marriage by deception: Tess is cut to the quick, and refuses Angel again.*

*Believing her evasion to be coyness, he woos her more subtly, and she knows she must weaken. After a last bid to renounce him, she agrees to drive the milk to the station with him.*

Jack Dollop (first seen in Chapter 21) has married a wealthy widow, who, fearing to lose him, fails to tell him until after the wedding that she has forfeited the money, under her first husband's will: 'the poor woman gets the worst o't'. The parallels with Tess's situation (now and later) are obvious, and the discussion of the woman's options painfully blunt: note Beck Knibbs' robust view that she would take no nonsense from her husband about

**Society**

'telling him beforehand anything whatsomdever about my first chap'. Comedy seems tragedy – again – to the self-conscious Tess.

Angel grows subtle, playing a 'more coaxing game' which uncomfortably echoes Alec's behaviour. Tess herself defines the triangle, feeling a 'certain moral validity' in her (sexual) 'union' with Alec: the idea that he is her 'real' husband occurs, later, to the men too. But she must accept Angel, and we begin to feel that she must also tell him the truth: Hardy ironically notes her trust in Angel as a man 'who would love and cherish and defend her, under any conditions, changes, charges, or revelations'. But will he?

# Chapter 30

*Intimate in the rainy darkness, Angel and Tess drive to the station. Tess tries to confess, but he interrupts: she loses courage and instead reveals her d'Urberville ancestry. Relieved, even pleased, Angel himself mentions Alec, her namesake. Agitated, Tess finally agrees to marry him.*

The tension keeps building towards a confession, as cross-references spotlight Tess's past: Angel picks blackberries for Tess, as Alec did strawberries; they are in a carriage together (though Angel, typically, drives safely). Tess's sexuality and impassioned kisses mock Angel's condescension towards her

**The past**

'inexperience'.

Tess tries four times to begin her story, but each time (creating suspense) she is prevented. Ironically, she fears that Angel will blame her for not telling him sooner: what can we anticipate of a wedding-night confession? Ironically, too, she uses her d'Urberville name – with its unspoken link to Alec – as a diversion. (Tess rightly thinks it 'unlucky': Angel wants to use it to make her more respectable, but it will, later, turn him against her.) Tess's continuing silence is again emphasised by Angel's mentioning Alec. Why does she accept his proposal at this moment? Could it be Angel's suggestion that by taking his name, she will 'escape' hers?

# Chapter 31

*Joan Durbeyfield writes, commanding Tess never to reveal her secret. Tess grows calm, in 'sublime trustfulness' and love of Angel, but is still haunted by regret and insecurity. The engagement is announced, and the dairymaids' generosity makes Tess resolve to tell Angel everything.*

Joan's advice is typically rambling, self-interested and irresponsible. (Given that Tess is bound to tell Angel sometime, do you feel that sooner is better than later?) Nevertheless, the letter allows Tess to give up her sense of responsibility for a while.

There is a period of precarious, 'ecstatic' happiness. Hardy examines at

length the nature of Tess's love for Angel. He is her masculine ideal – saintly, wise, considerate, protective (and thus, significantly, the opposite of Alec). But his love is 'inclined to the imaginative and ethereal', vulnerable to disillusionment. From summer mornings, their time together has moved into autumnal afternoons – beautiful, but shadowed. The demons

**Angel**

of Tess's past – doubt, fear, moodiness, care, shame – are only held at bay, like wolves outside the circle of light.

When the betrothal is discovered, the dairymaids are stunned, but bear Tess no ill will. Their generosity makes Tess feel that to marry Angel under false pretenses would be a betrayal of their suffering as well as his trust. She resolves to tell the truth at all costs.

# Chapter 32

*Since the milking is coming to an end, Tess sets a date for the wedding. Events speed up. Tess asks her mother for advice again, but there is no reply. Angel plans to learn flour-milling at Wellbridge – a d'Urberville seat. Tess remains insecure and fearful.*

Consider how Hardy maintains suspense, while making Tess's course seem inevitable. What, for example, does the 'brief glorification' of the gnats in the

sunlight tell us about Tess's moment of happiness? Economic factors (the release of female labour once milking is over) push Tess into setting a wedding date. Angel is also hurrying the wedding plans, and makes all the decisions. Tess is 'carried along upon the wings of the hours, without the sense of a

**Fate**

will'. Does any of this excuse her continued failure to tell Angel the truth?

Despite a surface acceptance, Tess's emotions are in turmoil. She is anxious when the banns are not read in church (Angel has instead got a licence, without telling her), despite fearing that somebody might stand up and forbid the marriage. She fears, with a mixture of fatalism and self-punishment, that her good fortune will be 'scourged out of' her by future ills. The chapter ends on an ominous note, as her wedding clothes (provided by Angel) remind her of the ballad of a mystic robe that changes colour to betray the guilt of an unfaithful wife.

## Chapter 33

*On Christmas Eve, Angel takes Tess for a day out in town. A Trantridge man recognises and insults her: Angel knocks him down. Shaken, Tess writes a letter of confession and puts it under his door. Angel says nothing. On their wedding day, she finds the letter under the carpet. After one last attempt to confess, she is 'whirled onward' to her wedding, and away from Talbothays.*

As events gather momentum, fate and the past intervene. By coincidence, a Trantridge man recognises Tess and makes a coarse joke about her being no 'maid' (virgin). Angel's violent indignation forces Tess to write her letter. After days of suspense, painfully hoping that he has forgiven her, she finds that it never reached him: pure chance, again. There is no more time. She makes a final attempt to confess, but is prevented by Angel, who is painfully aware (as we later find out) that he too has a confession to make.

Tess is 'whirled onward' through the 'critical hours' by the 'mastering tide of her devotion'. Her one desire is to make herself his, and  'then, if necessary, to die': a fulfilment delayed until the last chapters. The wedding scene is luminous with Tess's love, but full of ominous significance: the 'decayed' coachman; Tess's trust that Angel's loyalty is 'proof against all things'; his inability to appreciate the depth of her devotion. Afterwards, the omens become explicit. Tess learns of the d'Urberville coach and its 'dreadful crime', and immediately wonders whether she is more Alec's wife than Angel's: we make the prophetic connection. She fears that her idolatrous worship of Angel is ill-omened. And as they set off – for a d'Urberville farm – a cock crows: another note of doom. Is all this impressive – or excessive?

Fate

## Chapter 34

*Wellbridge is a depressing place with ominous d'Urberville portraits. Angel dresses Tess in heirloom jewels sent by his father. Finally, hand in hand, they sit by the fire. Angel confesses his past affair in London and – forgiving and relieved – Tess begins her own story...*

 The past catches up with both Tess and Angel. Wellbridge epitomises decayed d'Urberville fortunes. The portraits – suggestive of 'merciless treachery' – upset Tess, but Angel sees traces of them in her. The dead leaves of the past autumn are 'stirred to irritated resurrection' outside. Angel gives Tess jewels bequeathed by his godmother, whom he wistfully

The past

recalls prophesying a 'wondrous career' for him: wearing them, Tess looks a true d'Urberville. Against all this, there are touching hints, in the childish intimacy of sharing a home, of what might have been their future together.

Angel

Jonathan Kail, bringing their luggage, also brings news that Retty Priddle has tried to drown herself, Marian is drunk and Izz depressed. Tess feels they have had the punishment *she* deserves and resolves to 'pay to the uttermost farthing' by telling Angel everything. But he confesses first: he has kept a secret for fear of losing her. He has been on the point of speaking, but has put it off. He has feared blame for not speaking earlier. Why does Hardy take so much care here to make Angel seem the 'double' of Tess?

How do you feel about Angel at this point? Consider the tone of his confession, his assumption of Tess's forgiveness, his instant dismissal of the matter, his refusal to take seriously Tess's desire to confess. What is the effect on Tess of his dismissive statement that her sin can 'hardly be more serious' than his?

Look closely at the final paragraph, where Tess begins her confession. Hardy builds up resonant images from the most minute detail. What do you predict will happen next?

# Self-test (Questions) Phases Three & Four

### Uncover the plot
Delete two of the three alternatives given, to find the correct plot. Beware possible misconceptions and muddles.

Tess arrives at the Valley of Blackmoor/Emminster/Froom at the dairy of Mr Groby/Crick/Clare. She meets Marian/Retty/Izz Priddle and the others. Angel/Felix/Cuthbert Clare, a student/clergyman/dairyman notices her as a 'fallen/happy/virginal daughter of Nature'. They meet in the morning/evening/night through the autumn/summer/spring, until, during the skimming/harvest/milking, he embraces her. After visiting Marlott/Emminster/Talbothays, he proposes: Tess accepts/stalls/refuses, until a drive to the nearby town/station/flour mill. It is now spring/autumn/winter, and events hasten to a New Year/Christmas/May Day wedding. They go to Bramshurst/Wellbridge/Sandbourne, where Angel/Tess/Jonathan first makes a confession.

### Who? What? Why? When? Where? How?
1 Who says she would marry Angel 'and more' and why is this significant later?
2 Who are the two characters featured in Crick's funny stories?
3 What do the d'Urberville portraits 'suggest', and why is this disturbing?
4 What mainly attracts Tess to Angel?
5 What are Tess's first words in response to Angel's confession?
6 Why is the Talbothays community at 'the happiest of all positions in the social scale'?
7 Why does Tess refuse at first to marry Angel, and why does he think she does so?

8  Why does Angel not wish to wait until he has found a farm to marry Tess?
9  How do Retty, Izz and Marian respond to Angel's carrying them? And to his marriage?
10 How is Tess said to be different to the other dairymaids?

### Who said that?

From your knowledge of the characters in the novel, identify the following people:

1  Who said: 'She's brim full of poetry – actualised poetry, if I may use the expression'? Of whom?
2  Who said: 'She's too good for a dairymaid – I said so the very first day I zid her'? Of whom?
3  Who said: 'I shouldn't mind learning why – why the sun do shine on the just and unjust alike'?
4  Who said: 'The only pain to me was pain on his account, poor, foolish young man'? Of whom?
5  Who said: 'Well, I fancied, from the tone of your letters… that you were somehow losing intellectual grasp'. Of whom?

### What's the meaning of this?

These phases are a web of cross-references, omens, echoes and foreshadowings. Let's explore…

1  What is the significant aspect of the pollard willows (28), gnats (32) and gadflies (24)?
2  List three ill omens, recognised as such by the characters.
3  List four Biblical allusions in these phases, and sum up in a phrase what each suggests.
4  In what contexts is Alec mentioned to or by Angel (and not by Tess)? Why are they ironic?
5  What features of Jack Dollop's story seem significant to Tess?
6  On what two occasions do old d'Urberville properties crop up in these phases?
7  List four major coincidences in these phases.

### Human nature

List eight images of Tess as a plant or animal, and sum up in a word what each says about her.

### For everything there is a season

Match each event to the month in which it occurs:

| | |
|---|---|
| May | Angel carrying Tess across the flood |
| June | Angel's first proposal |
| July | Tess's arrival at Talbothays |
| August | The first embrace |
| September | The first meeting in the wild garden |
| October | Setting the wedding date |
| November | The wedding |
| December | Afternoon walks as a betrothed couple |

# Phase The Fifth: The Woman Pays

## Chapter 35

*Angel is stunned, unable to come to terms with the 'new' Tess. Escaping to the fields, followed meekly by Tess, Angel is emotionally controlled, but unrelenting. Later, outside her door, he hesitates, but the d'Urberville portraits mock him and harden him against Tess.*

Angel

Why does Angel react as he does? Is it just his deep-down conventionality that is revolted – or is it something more personal to Angel, his hopes and illusions? His main difficulty is the (true) perception that he has loved someone who never existed. Unable to accept his own limitations, he blames Tess for his disillusionment. He is self-centred, unable to look beyond the change in his universe. He is, as always, rigidly controlled, though with flashes of sarcasm and contempt. Do you feel sorry for him at all? He seems paralysed by genuine shock at first, and Hardy later focuses on the single tear that rolls down his face.

Note the intervention of the portrait, with its sexually vengeful air and resemblance to Tess. Is it fate, or Angel's inability to face his own limitations, that checks his compassionate impulse at this moment?

Tess

Compare Tess here with her behaviour in past crises. She is traumatised, crouching animal-like at Angel's feet, almost ugly in her terror. She is self-pitying and submissive, like a 'wretched slave', and follows Angel with 'dumb and vacant fidelity', like a whipped dog. Briefly, she finds the spirit to confront him with the irrationality of his anger. Look at the short speech 'What have I done…' This is perhaps the only time she says what really should be said to Angel. She fights back at his one flash of contempt, but then actually offers to drown herself if he wishes.

Is this all too melodramatic? What do you find convincing and unconvincing about these scenes?

## Chapter 36

*Angel and Tess maintain a painful normality, despite their estrangement. Angel is inflexible: he cannot live with Tess as his wife, but will not divorce her. Her last hopes gone, she submits to his judgement, and agrees to a separation: she will return home.*

Angel

The first paragraph sets the cold, devastated tone of this chapter, with its grotesque surface normality. Angel's intellectual pride makes him unable to cope with the collapse of his illusions, and he focuses his anger on Tess. A 'hard' streak of logic and determination make him utterly inflexible.

The 'ethereal' nature of his love favours separation: that way, he can avoid troublesome reality – 'with more animalism he would have been the nobler man', and stayed with Tess.

Yet Hardy suggests that Angel is soft at heart and might have been won

over, if Tess had not been so passively submissive. Angel himself is aware that she 'might have' used her physical attractions, and 'might have' pointed out that, abroad, no shame would reach their children. But she does not. Do you feel that Tess is throwing away a real chance here to take control of her destiny, or is Hardy encouraging you to feel that 'fate' is against her? Note how she dwells on death as a way of setting Angel free, linked with his later comment: 'How can we live together while that man lives?... If he were dead it might be different...'. Why does this sound ominous?

Fate

> The Woman Pays. Angel says he is guided by 'principle' – but note the double standard by which he forgets and forgives his own sexual transgression. Tess said 'Tis just the same!' – but to society it is not. Promiscuity is permitted in a man, as experience of the world, but it is a sin, with terrible social consequences, for a woman: Tess's family will be expelled from their home because she is not 'proper' (respectable). Do you think the same double standards exist today? What do you think of Hardy's understanding of women's struggles in society?

# Chapter 37

*Angel sleepwalks: mourning Tess as if she were dead, he carries her lovingly to an open coffin in the ruined Abbey. The next day, unaware, he takes her back to Talbothays for a brief, constrained visit. He leaves her – forbidding all contact except, in case of need, by letter – on her way back to Marlott.*

The sleepwalking scene is regarded as one of the least plausible but most effective in the novel, with its vivid, surreal quality. It shows the power of the feelings Angel is suppressing: both tenderness and mourning for a Tess – 'so good, so true' – he thinks he has lost. It also shows Tess's self-abandonment, her trust in Angel's protectiveness (not to be justified until the very end of the novel), and her strong attraction to death.

The return to Talbothays shows the painful change: the memories are

spoiled, the companions dispersed, the couple like 'waxen images'. Who is responsible for the separation? Hardy suggests that she could win Angel back, even now – but her 'mood of long-suffering' makes leaving easy for him. Her submission is partly pride, a 'reckless acquiescence in chance', daring fate to do its worst: an inheritance from the d'Urbervilles. As the

Tess

chapter ends, Hardy notes that Angel 'hardly knew that he loved her still'. Is there any hope here?

# Chapter 38

*Tess returns to Marlott, but her parents' shallow, self-centred reaction drives her away. Proudly pretending that Angel has asked her to join him, she gives them half the money he has left her, and leaves.*

Tess finds her marriage to be the gossip of the village. Her mother is accusing, hypocritical, self-pitying and fatalistic by turns: much as we expect. 'Sir John' is concerned only with the insult to the family name, and the opinion of the folk to whom he has just been boasting at the inn. Tess's alienation is reflected in the way the house at first seems the same, but she then sees that things have been shifted: 'There was no place here for her now'.

Hardy mentions the 'attacks of destiny', but shows that it is Tess's pride that makes her leave home, deceive her parents and give them half her money – setting up the events that will force her back to Alec.

**Fate**

# Chapter 39

*Angel, too, conceals the situation from his parents, saying that he is going to investigate Brazil before Tess joins him. Enduring their curiosity about her, he defends Tess's purity, but blames her in his heart.*

Angel's parents form a complete contrast to the Durbeyfields. They have

accepted his marriage and take a warm interest in Tess, unwittingly torturing Angel with their speculations. Mrs Clare is perceptive and concerned when Angel reacts emotionally to her affirmation that purity is more important than social refinement. Angel is in turmoil: he defends Tess as

**Society**

'spotless', yet is angry with her and has acute memories of her physical presence. Ironically, it is only now, faced by his parents' tolerance, that Angel feels he has wrecked his career by an unsuitable marriage, and feels not just a fool, but a 'failure' too.

Having admitted faults on both sides, Hardy here intervenes with a more biased voice. He has dwelt on the 'virtuous wife' (surely suggesting Tess) and emphasised words like 'pure', 'chaste', 'nature' and 'heart'. Finally, he pinpoints Angel's limitations, and how he clings to custom and convention, as the cause of the separation. He says that Tess's 'moral value' should be reckoned by intention ('tendency'), not by the results of her actions.

# Chapter 40

*Angel recklessly shocks Mercy Chant. Later, revisiting Wellbridge, he meets Izz Huett. Under extreme emotional pressure, he asks her to go with him to Brazil as his mistress. She agrees, but is forced to admit that no-one could love him like Tess. Angel comes to his senses, to Izz's grief. He is very close to returning to Tess, but is still too inflexible, and departs for Brazil.*

On the verge of Angel's departure from the scene, Hardy plants seeds of hope

Angel

in these glimpses of upheaval. Chance brings Izz to Wellbridge, a place and time of extreme pressure for Angel. Realising that she loves him, he feels trapped and frustrated that fate and society have left him no 'legitimate' options. He deliberately takes 'revenge' by defying social laws and his own principles by asking Izz to go to Brazil with him. But Izz's confession of Tess's love makes a huge impact on Angel: only his intellectual inflexibility ('if he was right at first, he was right now') makes him, finally, leave for Brazil.

Once again, 'the woman pays'. Angel tries to pass off his proposition as 'momentary levity', but the agonised Izz rightly rebukes him: 'it was no levity to me!'. Angel finally takes responsibility for the love of the dairymaids, but his compassion is not enough to redress their suffering.

# Chapter 41

*Tess has spent spring and summer working, but winter – and her family's demands – use up the money left by Angel. Seeking work, Tess sets out for the uplands where Marian now is. She is accosted by a stranger: the Trantridge man Angel had knocked down for insulting her. She flees to a plantation, where she finds wounded pheasants and puts them out of their misery.*

Tess is driven by various forces. Bad weather and the scarcity of work force

Fate

her into poverty. Coincidence guides her in the form of Marian's letter. Her beauty attracts unwanted attention, including an approach – with the impact of both fate and the past – from the Trantridge man who had recognised her before. (Do you think this is too outrageous a coincidence to justify the effect it achieves?)

Nature

But is Tess a pure victim? An image of her as a wild animal, driven by instinct, is explored further in the significant episode of the wounded pheasants. Tess identifies them as 'kindred sufferers', and wonders at men who 'destroy life' without compassion for 'their weaker fellows'. There are obvious parallels here with Tess. But she herself *contrasts* the birds' helpless victimhood with her ability to take responsibility for herself. We know that her pride prevented her from asking Angel's father for money, from telling her own family of her desertion, and from returning to Talbothays.

## Chapter 42

*Tess trudges on, protecting herself by mutilating her looks. The scarcity of work forces her to seek hard labour on arable land. Arriving at Flintcomb-Ash, she joins Marian, saying that Angel is abroad and she needs to supplement her allowance.*

Tess's self-mutilation represents a denial of her sexuality: she becomes 'a fieldwoman pure and simple', almost non-human. But underneath, there is 'pulsing life': note that although her colours are now grey and whitey-brown, faded by the elements, the red still stands out.

**Nature**

As Tess becomes part of the landscape, the location and season reflect her fortunes. We are now in the treeless, windblown uplands spread symbolically between Marlott and Talbothays: a desolate ('starve-acre') place. The weather is bad, but Tess does not mind its honest, impartial harshness. Hardy implies that people are more hurtful, through the cruelty of lust and the fragility of love (embodied by Alec and Angel).

This is an insight into the harsh realities of rural life in the last century: the scarcity of work, the rough labour on arable land, the dreariness of some areas, the exploitation of women's cheap labour. 'The woman pays', socially and emotionally, it seems. Consider Marian: reduced from dairy work to swede-hacking by her addiction to drink, caused by Angel's departure.

## Chapter 43

*In a harsh winter, the women endure the field-work, Marian by drinking and Tess by dreaming. When the snow comes, they switch to indoor reed-drawing. Izz arrives, and also Car Darch and her sister. Their employer turns out to be the Trantridge man, with a grudge against Tess. She learns of Angel's proposition to Izz, and resolves to write to him, but cannot finish the letter.*

The desolate land, harsh weather and hard labour are conveyed through a

**Nature**

wealth of detail, in a sequence, as winter advances. The style is vivid, but unusually simple and direct, ephasising the austerity of the women's lives. Consider how their dull doggedness is conveyed by: 'Marian said that they need not work any more. But if they did not work they would not be paid; so they worked on.'

**The past**

The companionship of Marian and Izz encourages Tess's dreams of Angel, but Alec's presence is also felt here. The crowding in of old faces – Car, whose hostility pushed Tess into Alec's arms, and the Trantridge man, who knows about Alec and was knocked down by Angel – emphasises the impossibility of escaping the past. Tess seems trapped 'like a bird caught in a clap-net' by the coincidences. Do you think Hardy has gone too far to create this effect?

Izz's tale leaves Tess desperately insecure – but she is silenced by the thought that Angel's rash act meant he could not care for her. If that is so, she does not wish to burden him with entreaties or protestations. Is this self-sacrifice, or pride? Do you sympathise with either?

# Chapter 44

*Insecure at Angel's silence, Tess goes hopefully to Emminster. The Clares are not at the vicarage, and she unluckily encounters Felix, Cuthbert and Mercy Chant. Their scornful remarks demoralise Tess and she trudges away – missing a vital chance of happiness. One the road, she stops to hear a fiery preacher: it is Alec.*

Tess hopes that the Clares will be able to 'enter into her heart-starved situation'. The greenness of the Vale of Blackmoor in the midst of winter reflects her hopes. The tragedy here is that her hopes are well-founded: Hardy says Tess is just the sort of person the Clares would reach out to. Her turning back is 'the greatest misfortune of her life'.

**Fate**

Why does Tess's courage fail? Hardy has built up the anxiety, especially at the Cross-in-Hand and the deserted vicarage, with its tapping ivy and piece of blood-stained paper. Self-condemnation, hopelessness and pride all contribute, too. But Hardy emphasises the role of fate as the phase draws to a close. Chance lets Tess meet the wrong Clares and overhear their remarks. Chance makes them find, and scorn, the boots she has put aside to look respectable. Chance makes her stop to hear the preacher. The return of the past to haunt her is signalled by the reappearance of the man with the paint pot. Are you surprised by the fact that the preacher is Alec d'Urberville?

> Note how Hardy brings together all the religious figures here: the narrow-minded brothers, the unsuitably named 'Mercy', the compassionate parents, plus the fiery preacher and the painter. The religious theme prepares us for the next phase: the Convert.

# Self-test (Questions) Phase Five

### Uncover the plot
Delete two of the three alternatives given, to find the correct plot. Beware possible misconceptions and muddles.

Angel's face has 'changed/fallen/withered'. He cannot forgive/love/reject Tess: she is a wicked/different/wronged person. By day, he is distraught/loving/controlled, but one night he cries/rages/sleepwalks. He decides on divorce/separation/reconciliation, and after visiting Emminster/Talbothays/Trantridge, sends Tess home. Joan is typically sympathetic/vexed/calm. Angel leaves for London/Brazil/Wellbridge, having tried to take Izz/Tess/Mercy with him. In February/May/October, Tess runs out of patience/money/pride and seeks Angel/Alec/work at Flintcomb-Ash/Chalk-Newton/Port Bredy with Marian/Izz/Retty. Visiting the Durbeyfields/Clares/Cricks for news, she meets Angel/Cuthbert/John and his brother. Turning back, she hears a gossip/preacher/singer. It is Angel/Mr Clare/Alec.

### Who? What? Why? When? Where? How?
1　Who does Tess overhear talking about her at Emminster?
2　Who is listening to Alec preach?
3　What is 'the greatest misfortune' of Tess's life?
4　What three arguments does Tess use to Angel in her one brief fight against his rejection?
5　What had been Tess's plan to set Angel free, if necessary, and what is her only option now?
6　Why does Angel say he cannot live with Tess, after her confession?
7　Why does Angel change his mind about taking Izz as his mistress to Brazil?
8　Why does Tess decide to write to Angel, and then visit Emminster?
9　How does Tess's employer at Flintcomb-Ash treat her, and why?
10　How does the money Angel left for Tess run out?

### Who is this?
From your knowledge of the characters in the novel, identify the following people:
1　Who 'thought he knew [life] as a practical man; though perhaps he did not, even yet'?
2　Who takes Tess's ruin 'as she would have taken a wet holiday or a failure in the potato crop'?
3　Who is 'a soul who could feel for kindred sufferers as much as for herself'?
4　Who says: 'Since she is pure and chaste she would have been refined enough for me'?

### Where are we now?
Changes of location emphasise the change in Tess's life. Let's explore…
1　What places does Tess revisit? Find a quote to sum up how each has changed.
2　What is significant about Angel's return to Wellbridge?
3　What are the main features of the land at Flintcomb-Ash? What does it contrast with?
4　What characters from Tess's past have moved in this phase: from where, to where?

**Past and done?**

What previous incidents or lines in the novel do the following remind you of?

1 Angel sees traces of Tess in the d'Urberville portraits (35)
2 Angel sleepwalks with Tess (37)
3 Tess is dressed up in her best clothes by Marian and Izz to visit Emminster (44)
4 Tess has a 'loss of courage at the last and critical moment' (44)

**Open quotes**

Complete the following useful quotes:

1 'Some might risk the odd paradox that with more animalism...' (36)
2 Tess 'had learnt too well, for [her] years, of the dust and ashes of things, of the...' (42)
3 'With all his attempted independence of judgement, this advanced and well-meaning young man...' (39)
4 'And she went her way without knowing that the greatest misfortune of her life was...' (54)

**The woman pays**

How do we see women paying in this phase?

# Phase The Sixth: The Convert

# Chapter 45

*Alec, on seeing Tess, falters in his preaching and rushes after her. He explains how he was converted by Mr Clare after the death of his mother, but Tess does not believe his conversion is real. Alec, disturbed by Tess, makes her swear on the Cross-in-Hand not to tempt him. Afterwards, a shepherd explains that it is no Holy Cross, but a place of torture.*

**Religion**

At first glance, Alec is 'palpably a converted man'. Tess notes in detail the complete 'transformation' of his appearance and manner but she does not entirely believe in this conversion. Do you? Are you convinced by the semi-clerical dress and pious speech, given Alec's tendency to adopt disguises? Note the flashes of his old self: his description of his conversion as 'a jolly new idea', his lurking resentment, his lingering gaze on Tess. He seems sincere but insecure in his new role, calming inner turmoil by reading Mr Clare's letter.

**The past**

Tess reacts with disbelief, and with bitterness that Alec can ruin her life and then escape judgement. She confronts him with spirit, but his old power soon asserts itself, making her ashamed of her sexuality: Alec represents her guilt. She despairs at the sense of 'an implacable past which still engirdled her' and which she cannot escape. Note the echoes of the past: Alec's mother, Tess's child, scriptures painted in red. Hardy reminds us of the links between Tess and Alec, while keeping Angel in our minds. What is the effect of the Cross-in-Hand at this point? Or Tess's recognition that: 'Bygones would never be complete bygones till she was a bygone herself'?

# Chapter 46

*Alec turns up at Flintcomb-Ash and asks Tess to marry him. She refuses, confessing that she is already married. But Alec's feelings for her have reawakened. Tess starts another letter to Angel. Alec appears again at her lodging, and they discuss religion. He has broken a preaching engagement to see her, his conversion crumbling under temptation.*

Hardy builds up suspense with Alec's gradual approach. He is identified by his costume at first. What might this say about his new rôle? Other warnings come in flashes of his old capriciousness, irony and lust. He is clearly under temptation. So is Tess: persecuted by Groby, she wonders what it would be like to marry Alec and be 'lifted out of subjection'. The triangle has intensified now that Alec knows about Angel: what is Tess afraid of, that she tries to write to Angel again?

Alec

In the second visit, we see and hear Alec's piety crumbling. He explains that his conversion was just a 'whimsical' search for a 'new sensation' in the shock of his mother's death. In the religious discussion, Alec's renewed animality clashes with Angel's intellect. Alec points out that Tess's mind is 'enslaved': both forms of male domination have reduced her. Ironically it is Alec, though contemptuous of women, who sees Tess as 'unsmirched in spite of all'.

> The subtle ironies of the phase title, 'The Convert', have begun to emerge. Angel was converted out of his father's faith. Tess was converted by Angel. His father's convert, Alec, is now being de-converted by Tess. Alec himself, in the sinister last lines of the chapter, appreciates the irony of Angel's views paving the way for his wife's seducer to renew his attentions.

# Chapter 47

*Tess is working on the exhausting threshing machine when Alec reappears. He tells her that she has made him renounce his faith, and asks her to leave her absent husband for him. Tess strikes him.*

Society

The threshing machine epitomises the threat inherent in the coming of technology. Hardy has acknowledged the harshness of field labour, but the machine is presented as a monstrous and brutalising force, completely alien to nature and humanity. It is red and black, tyrannical and 'inexorable', reminiscent of hell or the torture chamber. The engine man is dark, isolated, unseeing and uncaring, a servant of 'fire and smoke'.

Alec, too, is inexorable. This time he is a figure in a fashionable suit: the

Alec

clash of 'dandy' and 'ranter pa'son' confuses Marian. But it is the old Alec, back to his exaggerated villainy: curses, cynical laughter, recklessness, violence. Do you think his parting shot ('Remember, my lady, I was your master once; I will be your master again') too melodramatic? Or do you sense a real danger? Consider the omens: Tess's drawing blood – linked to her ancestral past, and future; her defiance, like a sparrow 'before its captor twists its neck'; her fatalistic cry: 'Once victim, always victim: that's the law.'

## Chapter 48

*At the end of the day, Alec turns up again as the rat-catching begins. More subtle now, he sympathises with Tess's exhaustion and offers to help her family. At the mention of the children, she almost breaks down, but refuses to take anything from him. That night she writes a long, passionate appeal to Angel to return before something terrible happens.*

Tess is already weakened by the threshing machine, described even more

Tess

graphically here, when Alec turns up. Although he appears as 'a friend', he takes his cue from the hunting down of the rats in the hay rick. Tess is at her most vulnerable to his temptations: she desperately needs rest from her labours, but is more anxious about provision for the children. The force of this temptation makes her finally write to Angel. She begs him to return, or to let her go to him: she is being 'pressed', and fears what 'an accident' and her own defencelessness might lead to. The letter is deeply impassioned. You may also think it rather sophisticated in style: why might Hardy wish to concentrate on Tess's sensitivity here?

## Chapter 49

*Tess's letter is on its way. Meanwhile, in Brazil, Angel has been ill and the farming disastrous. Experience teaches him tolerance and his heart softens towards Tess. Back in England, she is hopeful – but her sister Liza-Lu arrives with news that their mother is sick.*

Hardy maintains the suspense in a spiral of scenes which seem to be converging on the moment when Angel will receive Tess's letter. We see the letter arrive at Emminster; a flashback to the softening of Angel's heart in Brazil; back to the present, with Angel prepared for Tess's letter, just being forwarded; and back to Tess, hopefully preparing for his return. But chance breaks in at this point.

Angel's development is almost complete. Illness and disaster have matured him, and he has realised that motives are more important than actions. A

Angel

'large-minded stranger' (met by chance and dying suddenly) teaches him a tolerance born of wide experience. Angel confesses his own narrow-mindedness and, remembering Tess's love, realises her true worth (including her d'Urberville name).

# Chapter 50

*Tess arrives in Marlott. The family are in a poor state, and she takes charge. She is in the allotment when Alec appears. He offers again to help the family, but Tess refuses. On her way home, she is met with the news that her father is dead.*

Tess's journey to Marlott is dark, under the 'steely stars', through ancient forests and memories of innocence. What do you sense the outcome of her visit will be?

Alec

Hardy carefully establishes the allotment scene: shifting light and smoke, quiet sounds, a whisper of spring in the air. A man in a smockfrock works beside Tess: suddenly the fire flares up and there is Alec, pitchfork in hand. This is explicitly devilish: Alec says he is Satan come in disguise to tempt Eve. Indeed he plays on Tess's greatest weakness by offering to help the children.

We last see John Durbeyfield planning to get local 'antiqueerians' to set up a fund to maintain him – like other 'old ruins'. This is comic, until we learn that the lease on the house lapses with his death, and he has made no provision for the family. Why does Hardy add a final reference here to the d'Urbervilles, destiny, and 'the rhythm of change'?

# Chapter 51

*The Durbeyfields are being expelled, no longer respectable in the eyes of the village. Alec turns up again, and offers to lodge them at Trantridge, but Tess refuses: they have taken rooms in Kingsbere. He reaches out to her, she reacts violently and Alec storms off. Tess finally realises that Angel has been unjust. She dashes off a brief, angry letter and despairs.*

Here we have Hardy's wistful account of change in the rural community. The

Society

variety and stability of village life is being eroded. The artisans and 'better-informed' folk, the preservers of village traditions, are effectively banished to the large towns as their leases expire, making way for more productive use of the land. The remaining population are farm labourers who annually migrate from farm to farm on Lady Day.

The past

We return to the noose tightening around Tess. The past is acutely present: Tess's ruin has sealed the family's expulsion by the self-righteous villagers; they are going to Kingsbere, site of the d'Urberville vaults: the man with the paint pot reappears. Alec dwells on the past, but also offers a future that puts pressure on Tess. Note the foreshadowing: when Alec appears Tess thinks she hears a coach (the d'Urberville Coach with its rape and murder, omen of death); she again reacts violently to Alec. Meanwhile, Hardy builds up small, sad details: the drizzling rain, the web of a starved spider, the children's innocent faith.

The chapter ends with Tess's feeling that 'in a physical sense, Alec alone was her husband'.

# Chapter 52

*It is Lady Day, and the rural families are on the move, among them the Durbeyfields. Tess runs into Marian and Izz. The family arrive at Kingsbere, but there are no rooms and they have to camp at the church. Alec turns up again, ominously confident: Tess despairs. Marian and Izz write to Angel, warning him that his wife is threatened.*

The vulnerability of the family – 'only women', not regular labourers, not hired or required anywhere – is emphasised to maintain our sense of the pressure on Tess. Alec has a complete, confident ascendancy. Tess is helpless, her strength eroded by circumstance, desperation and exhaustion. Why does Hardy work so hard to make this point?

The past

The ruined glory of the old church symbolises Tess's ancestral past and clashes ironically with the homely pile of Durbeyfield household items outside it. Note how relentlessly the name of d'Urberville is repeated – culminating in the appearance of the false d'Urberville, Alec: 'The old order changeth'. Alec appears yet again as an unrecognised figure, this time as an effigy on a tomb. It is the last time we see him. And we leave Tess among the ancient d'Urberville graves, longing for death. The next, and final, phase is called 'Fulfilment'. What kind of fulfilment do you see for Tess?

Society

The portrait of general migration is the last in a series of set-pieces in this phase about country life in the last century. Consider how Tess's fate has been shaped by social and economic factors. Have you found this aspect of the novel successful and realistic?

# Self-test (Questions) Phase Six

**Uncover the plot**
Delete two of the three alternatives given, to find the correct plot. Beware possible misconceptions and muddles.

Alec says religion was a 'profound/moving/jolly new idea' after his horse's/mother's/child's death. Disturbed by Tess's disbelief/looks/forgiveness, he makes her swear not to tempt/reject/follow him. Tess is threshing/turnip slicing/reed drawing when he appears at Marlott/Evershead/Flintcomb-Ash and asks her to leave/live with/marry him. Later, he keeps/breaks/forgets a preaching engagement and discusses religion/Angel/marriage with Tess. Alec blames God/Tess/Angel for his backsliding, and asks her to return to him/Angel/Marlott: she hits/kisses/ignores him. He offers to help her husband/family/friends: scornful/indifferent/tempted, she writes to Joan/Angel/Mr Clare, who, meanwhile, feels 'love/faith/hope renascent'. Abraham/Joan/Liza-Lu brings news that John/Joan/Abraham is very ill. When John dies, the family are secure/homeless/welcome. They go to Wellbridge/Bramshurt/Kingsbere, where Angel/Alec/Groby turns up again.

**Who? What? Why? When? Where? How?**
1   Who does Tess encounter on the way to Kingsbere in the waggon?
2   Who writes letters, and to whom, in this phase?
3   What three main elements of truth are there in Alec's comments on Tess and Angel?
4   What does Alec use to put pressure on Tess to return to him?
5   What is the religion that Angel has taught Tess?
6   When are work contracts entered into and when do the workers move?
7   Why does Alec not despise Tess, of all the women he has known?
8   Why has Alec converted to Christianity?
9   How do John and Joan Durbeyfield each put added pressure on Tess to return to Alec?
10  How does the 'large-minded stranger' in Brazil influence Angel?

**Who is this?**
From your knowledge of the characters in the novel, identify the following people:
1   Who 'had mentally aged a dozen years'?
2   Who 'had not been shining examples either of temperance, soberness, or chastity'?
3   Who says: 'Remember, my lady, I was your master once. I will be your master again!'?
4   Who says: 'I shall not cry out. Once victim, always victim. That's the law!'?
5   Who 'was in the agricultural world, but not of it. He served fire and smoke'?

**Before and after**
In this phase, past and future collide with the present. Let's explore…
1   What two recurring legends are completed in this phase? What are they associated with?
2   How is Tess's first violent reaction to Alec linked to both past and future?
3   What omens of judgement and death accompany Tess's last meeting with Alec at Marlott?
4   What aspects of this phase recall Phase the First: The Maiden?
5   What aspects of this phase recall Phase the Second: Maiden No More?
6   How does Hardy keep Angel present, despite his absence from the action?

7  List four points where the d'Urbervilles are explicitly recalled.
8  What two major changes in rural life do we witness in this phase?
9  Complete the following useful quotes:
   (a) 'Bygones would never be complete bygones...' (45)
   (b) 'So do flux and reflux...' (50)
   (c) 'The old order...' (52)

**Costume drama**
In what 'form' or 'figure' do we first see Alec, in his various unexpected appearances?

**Phased out**
Who is 'The Convert' in this phase?

---

# Phase The Seventh: Fulfilment

## Chapter 53

*Angel returns to Emminster, shocking his parents by his worn appearance. Receiving Tess's last, angry letter, he hesitates to see her, and writes to Marlott instead. Joan eventually promises to inform him if Tess returns, but re-reading Tess's previous loving letter, Angel decides to seek her.*

Angel is a changed man. Physically worn, he looks like a painting of the dead  Christ: no longer the ethereal angel, but part of suffering humanity. He humbly accepts Tess's reproaches and recognises his disloyalty and failure to judge her 'by the will rather than by the deed'. He has also grown sensitive, considering Tess's feelings and realising that pride has led her into poverty and suffering.

Angel

Hardy builds up the suspense: what *is* happening to Tess? Everything involves Angel in further delay and waiting, while the repetition of the various letters reminds us of the pressure Tess was under when we left her.

## Chapter 54

*Angel seeks Tess at Flintcomb-Ash, then at Marlott, where he is referred to Joan's new home. She is evasive, but finally sends him to Sandbourne.*

As Angel seeks Tess, we are – like him – reminded constantly of her and of  the events that put her under pressure from Alec at each location. The new Angel experiences all this with acute sensitivity and longing: he can hardly bear to be in Marlott, with its 'dim ghosts'. In a poignant gesture, symbolic of his acceptance of Tess's past, he pays for the vainly superior

Angel

gravestone of John Durbeyfield. Note the echo of the first chapter: 'How are the mighty fallen'.

We also see Joan for the last time. Now a 'respectable widow', she attains some dignity: she reproaches Angel for his conduct to Tess and admits that she herself never really knew her. Her reluctance for Angel to find Tess rings warning bells, as does her comment that she is well provided for. By whom?

# Chapter 55

*Angel arrives at the fashionable seaside resort of Sandbourne and traces Tess to a stylish lodging house. He humbly begs her to come to him, but he is too late. A shocked Tess explains that she has returned to Alec. She asks Angel to leave her, and, traumatised, he wanders away.*

The suspense and irony of Angel's search deepens. Sandbourne is new, unnatural, fashionable, totally alien to Tess: what is she doing here? Angel seeks her by the name of Clare, then Durbeyfield, before getting word of 'Mrs d'Urberville'. He is pleased that she is using her married status and 'real' name (he never knew the name of her seducer – Mr d'Urberville). At the lodging house, he fears Tess is a servant, but she appears richly dressed. What do *you* think has happened?

Has your attitude to Angel changed by now? We see his longing for Tess,  his heart pounding at her footsteps, the touching vulnerability of his fear that he is so altered she will not love him any more. His first words are not to offer forgiveness, but to ask for it. His old fluent speech is now broken. When the truth sinks in, he is stricken, but his reaction to *this* confession – in dramatic contrast to the last – is: 'Ah – it is my fault!'

Angel

This is the worst crisis of Tess's life. Her manner is unnatural, shocked, as if she is in a nightmare, and she tells her story in a disconnected, almost manic manner: note the repetitions of 'you did not come' and 'He… He… He–' until 'He has won me back to him'. Tess is in a dressing gown (grey: a symbolic colour shift) and Alec is 'upstairs': this is as close as Hardy can get to saying that Tess is his mistress. She has accepted the situation with

Tess

reckless, hopeless submission ('I didn't care what he did wi' me') and it seems to Angel as if her body is drifting like a corpse, her soul elsewhere. How does this affect your view of Tess?

Tess's first words are: 'It is too late!' Why do you think she wants Angel to go away? What can she not bear, that Angel's presence makes her face?

# Chapter 56

*Mrs Brooks, the landlady, has overheard their conversation. Eavesdropping, she hears Tess and Alec arguing, then Tess leaving the house. Downstairs, she notices a growing stain on the ceiling. Blood. Alec has been stabbed through the heart.*

The events in this chapter are narrated through the ears and eyes of Mrs Brooks, with a detached and yet vivid – almost cinematic – effect. We see only what she sees through the keyhole, and hear only snatches of conversation, notably Tess's anguished, disjointed accusation of Alec, and her poignant self-blame for Angel's haggard appearance. Mrs Brooks retreats, and we hear only small, tense sounds. Then we see, on the white ceiling, the spreading red stain: the final fulfilment of Tess's colour motif. Hardy heightens the suspense through Mrs Brooks' gradual investigation: the dripping sound, the breakfast table with its missing carving knife.

Why is the murder seen through a stranger's eyes? Do you still feel sympathy for Tess?

# Chapter 57

*Angel waits for a train, then sets out on foot. Tess comes running after him and tells him, with relief and contentment, that she has killed Alec. Angel responds with absolute tenderness, vowing to stand by her. They wander into the country and take refuge in an empty mansion.*

Angel's trauma is highlighted by the intrusion of the 'normal' world in a telegram announcing Cuthbert's engagement to Mercy Chant, a shocking irrelevancy at this point.

When Tess catches up with Angel, she seems on the edge of madness. She is free of any sense of guilt for the murder: she has killed Alec so that Angel will forgive her and love her again. (Remember Angel's former words of rejection: 'If he were dead it might be different'.) She is disarmingly innocent, content and trustful. Hardy hints at mental confusion: she idolises Angel, still, as the only man who has ' believed in her as pure'.

Tess

Angel finally offers Tess unreserved love and protection, whatever she may have done (or not done: he is not sure until the police arrive that her story is not an hallucination).

Despite the possibility of pursuit hanging over them, they are curiously at peace, childishly carefree. The weather is 'serenely bright' and Bramshurst Court old-fashioned and secluded. What is Hardy doing here? What does he suggest by the four-poster bed and falling darkness?

> The phase title is 'Fulfilment'. In this chapter, Tess has fulfilled her fate by killing Alec. Angel has fulfilled all her hopes of him. And it is suggested that they have at last fulfilled – consummated – their marriage. What final fulfilment do you think awaits Tess?

# Chapter 58

*Tess and Angel spend a happy week in the peaceful house. The caretaker finds them sleeping, and though she does not disturb them, they feel they must leave. Walking all day across country, they stumble on Stonehenge in the dark. Tess asks Angel to look after her sister Liza-Lu. At dawn, the police close in and find Tess sleeping. Angel is helpless. Tess awakes, and steps forward with the words 'I am ready'.*

Tess has finally forgotten the past, and is fatalistic about the future: 'What must come will come'. She still longs for death, but no longer in desperation: she merely feels that her happiness – in Angel's love – cannot last, and she wants to die before she loses it. Hardy is preparing us to accept the inevitable. The intimacy and seclusion of Bramshurst reinforces the mood of peaceful acceptance, while the scant narrative emphasises its brevity: time is flying.

**Fate**

Stonehenge is a fitting destination for Tess's last journey: natural, pagan and 'older than the d'Urbervilles'. Tess feels 'at home'.

She asks Angel to marry Liza-Lu, whom she sees as an ideal version of herself. This is a rather sentimental twist, but perhaps Hardy wants us to feel, as Tess does, that she, and her love for Angel, will somehow continue. There is no sentiment, however, in Angel's refusal to give Tess the comforting answer to her question: will they be together after death? Is this Angel's last failure, or unflinching honesty to a truth that Hardy cannot let us escape?

Tess is glad to die: 'This happiness could not have lasted... and now I shall not live for you to despise me.' She has learnt 'the fragility of love' too well. Yet her acceptance allows us to leave her with a sense, not of outrage, but of 'Fulfilment'.

# Chapter 59

*Angel and Liza-Lu walk through the city of Wintoncester to an ugly tower at the top of the hill. They wait and watch. A black flag is raised. After a prayer, they walk on, hand in hand.*

It is a bright summer morning. Nature has abandoned Tess: she is dying in a city, with the sun smiling 'pitilessly' on. We watch Angel and Liza-Lu as if they were strangers: the tone is detached, perhaps numbed. For once, Tess is not present at all. A black flag is the single, poignant signal of her death.

**Nature**

Consider your response to the last paragraph of the book. Critics have found the reference to the 'President of the Immortals' heavy-handed. But might this be deliberate? Hardy invokes uncaring 'Justice' (his ironic inverted commas), the malicious gods, the unknowing d'Urbervilles, the helpless prayers of the watchers: society, fate, the past, God. But the flag continues to wave. There are no answers for us in any of these things. Only Angel and Liza-Lu, hand in hand, arising and going on.

**The past**

What emotions are you left with as you close the book?

# Self-test (Questions) Phase Seven

**Uncover the plot**

Delete two of the three alternatives given, to find the correct plot. Beware possible misconceptions and muddles.

Angel returns to Talbothays/Emminster/Trantridge, looking ill/prosperous/excited. His parents give him Tess's first/second/third letter. He first writes/rides/walks to Marlott, but after a day's/week's/month's delay, he sets out to seek Tess/Alec/Joan. Tess is well remembered at Flintcomb-Ash/Marlott/Kingsbere, but Groby/Tringham/Joan finally sends him to Shaston/Marlott/Sandbourne. He finds Tess as Mrs Clare/Durbeyfield/d'Urberville, dressed in white/grey-white/red. She says: 'It is all over/too much/too late': she is Alec's wife/mistress/servant. Later, Mrs Crick/Kaill/Brooks finds Alec beaten/stabbed/strangled. Tess catches Angel at the hotel/station/high road and says: 'I owed it to you/him/Sorrow.' At last, 'love/disbelief/tenderness' is 'absolutely dominant' in Angel. They rest at Wellbridge/Evershead/Bramshurst for a day/week/month, then flee to Stonehenge/Cross-in-Hand/Wintoncester, where Tess is executed/arrested/freed. On a May/September/July morning, a white/red/black flag is raised, watched by Angel and Tess/Liza-Lu/Izz.

**Who? What? Why? When? Where? How?**

1 Who 'witnesses' the murder of Alec, and Tess and Angel's flight?
2 Whom does Tess wish Angel to marry after she is gone and why?
3 What news does Angel get just as he is leaving his hotel in Sandbourne?
4 What five things do you notice that reflect the change in Angel?
5 Where do Alec and Tess respectively meet their deaths?
6 When does Angel realise that Tess has really killed Alec, and why has he not been sure?
7 Why does Tess finally hate Alec, and why does she say she has killed him?
8 Why is Tess ready to die?
9 How does Angel track Tess down to Sandbourne?
10 How do John and Joan Durbeyfield last appear in the novel?

**Who is this?**

From your knowledge of the characters in the novel, identify the following people:

1 Who is 'so good and simple and pure', and according to whom?
2 Who says: 'I will protect you by every means in my power, dearest love, whatever you may have done'?
3 Who is 'still a handsome woman, in the garb of a respectable widow'?
4 Whose breathing is 'quick and small, like that of a lesser creature than a woman'?
5 Who says: 'This happiness could not have lasted. It was too much'?

**This is your life**

As Tess's life draws to a close, many strands of the past are drawn together. Why might the following sound familiar?

1 Angel wonders about the d'Urberville coach: was there a violent streak in the family? (57)
2 Angel goes from Emminster, past the Cross-in-Hand, to Flintcomb-Ash (54)
3 John Durbeyfield's gravestone carries the words: 'How are the mighty fallen' (54)
4 Angel finds Tess dressed up in finery, but with her old 'fluty' voice (55)

5 Alec's blood drips red through the white ceiling (56)
6 Tess believes she can get Angel back by killing Alec (57)
7 Tess is surrounded by the police while sleeping on an altar (58)

**Familiar themes**

What main themes of the novel are raised by the following?

1 Tess is arrested at Stonehenge: 'older than the centuries, older than the d'Urbervilles' (58)
2 From the tower, you could see 'landscape beyond landscape, till the horizon was lost in the radiance of the sun hanging above it' (59)
3 At Bramshurst: 'Within was affection, union, error forgiven: outside was the inexorable' (58)
4 Angel refuses to say he believes that he and Tess will meet again after death (58)
5 The last paragraph of the novel

**Phased out**

In what sense are the events of this phase a 'fulfilment'?

# Self-test (Answers) Phases One & Two

Numbers in brackets refer to the chapters in which the answers can be found.

**Uncover the plot**
In May, in the Vale of Blackmoor, John Durbeyfield (a dealer) discovers he is a d'Urberville. Tess is urged to go to Trantridge to claim kinship with Mrs d'Urberville, and when Prince is killed she agrees. At The Slopes, she meets Alec, who offers her work as a fowl-keeper. After a dance at Chaseborough, Tess gets into a fight with the Queen of Spades: Alec 'rescues' her but in the foggy September night, seduces her. She returns home carrying his child. Tess recovers her spirits, but then Sorrow dies. Some time later, Tess resolves to leave.

**Who? What? Why? When? Where? How?**
1  Parson Tringham: sets everything in motion (1). Man with paint pot: makes her ashamed (12). Churchgoers: drive her away from church (13). Parson: refuses to baptise her baby (14).
2  Angel, Felix, Cuthbert: three brothers (1)
3  Roses and strawberries (5). A new horse and toys for the children (11)
4  Common sense; desire for usefulness and independence; familiar surroundings; girls' friendliness (14)
5  John's drunkeness; Tess's lack of sleep; the speed of the mailcart; bad luck; Tess's 'reverie' (4)
6  Early May (spring) – a year after Sorrow's death (15)
7  Responsibility for a new horse; children crying; Joan labouring; father coughing (6)
8  Sorrow was not properly baptised, and – having been refused entry to the house by John – the parson could not accept that the 'irregular' baptism was 'necessary' (14)
9  Plans her going to Trantridge (4); dresses her to attract Alec (7); has not warned her about men (12); has given Tess her beauty (7)
10  Dread, then succumbing to trickery, then being 'stirred to confused surrender', then despising him (12)

**Who is this?**
1  Joan Durbeyfield (5)
2  The man with the paint pot (12)
3  Tess (2)
4  John Durbeyfield (6)
5  Alec d'Urberville (5)
6  Angel Clare (2)

**Looking ahead**
1  Angel will leave Tess, having failed to consummate the marriage (37)
2  Tess will murder Alec (56)
3  She is sleeping when Alec finds her (11) and when the police come for her (58)
4  Alec will force himself, and early womanhood/motherhood, on Tess (11)
5  Tess will never meet Mr Clare (Angel's father), although she tries (44)

**Ironic, isn't it?**
1  The next time he sees her, she is a 'maiden no more'
2  Alec is 'roving' outside, waiting to pose as her protector
3  Tess is in trouble precisely because of putting the family above herself
4  Alec will 'die bad': murdered by Tess, whom he has seduced to be his mistress

5 At the same time, she looks forward to visiting the d'Urberville seat near Talbothays

**Pointers**
1 Tess's first meeting with Alec (5)
2 Tess's seduction (11)

# Self-test (Answers) Phases Three & Four

### Uncover the plot
Tess arrives at the Valley of Froom at the dairy of Mr Crick. She meets Retty Priddle and the others. Angel Clare, a dairyman, notices her as a 'virginal daughter of Nature'. They meet in the morning through the summer, until during the milking he embraces her. After visiting Emminster, he proposes: Tess refuses, until a drive to the nearby station. It is now autumn, and events hasten to a New Year wedding. They go to Wellbridge, where Angel first makes a confession.

### Who? What? Why? When? Where? How?
1 Izz Huett (21). She will later agree to go to Brazil as Angel's mistress (40)
2 William Dewey (17), Jack Dollop (21, 29)
3 'Merciless treachery' and 'arrogance to the point of ferocity'. They resemble Tess (34)
4 His love is 'disinterested, chivalrous, protective' – the opposite of Alec's demands (31)
5 'O, Angel – I am almost glad – because now *you* can forgive *me*!' (34)
6 It is above neediness, but below pretentious ambitions that 'cramp natural feeling' (24)
7 Fear of hurting him when he discovers her 'shame'. He thinks it suddenness, then a sense of social inferiority, then coyness (27-29)
8 A 'tinge of recklessness'; the end of milking work; wanting to keep Tess by him to prepare her to meet his parents (32)
9 Retty: 'a bunch of hysterics'; attempted suicide. Izz: 'sensibly and calmly'; depression. Marian: 'like a sack of meal'; drink (23, 34)
10 'More finely formed, better educated... more woman'; 'deeper-passioned' (21)

### Who said that?
1 Angel (26) of Tess
2 Crick (32) of Tess
3 Tess (19)
4 Mr Clare (26) of Alec
5 Felix (25) of Angel

### What's the meaning of this?
1 Tortured out of natural shape (like Tess by conscience); brief glory (like Tess's happiness); maddening (like passion to Angel)
2 The mystic robe (33). The d'Urberville coach (26,33). The afternoon cock crow (34)
3 River of Life: hope/purity (16). Adam and Eve: purity threatened by temptation (20,27). Mary Magdalen: a fallen woman forgiven (20). Last Day: judgement (34)

4    Mr Clare's failures (26). Mr Clare's compassion (27). A namesake of Tess (30). Hopes of Alec's conversion will (briefly) be fulfilled. Angel does not know that Alec is Tess's seducer

5    A seducer (21). Deceived by a wife who has witheld a secret, to do with her previous man, until after the wedding (29)

6    They pass one driving to the station (30). Angel chooses Wellbridge for the honeymoon (32)

7    Angel and Tess at Talbothays together; 'Mr Clare of Emminster' is Angel's father; Mr Clare's meeting with Alec; Jack Dollop's story mirroring Tess's

### Human nature
Fly on a billiard table: insignificance (16). Tree transplanted: blossoming (20). Snake: sensuality (27). Sunned cat: sensuality (27). Withered plant: sensitivity (27). Wildflower: innocence (28). Poised leopard: sexuality (30). Trapped bird: vulnerability (31)

### For everything there is a season
Angel carrying Tess across the flood – July
Angel's first proposal – September
Tess's arrival at Talbothays – May
The first embrace – August
The first meeting in the wild garden – June
Setting the wedding date – November
The wedding – December
Afternoon walks as a betrothed couple – October

# Self-test (Answers) Phase Five

**Uncover the plot**
Angel's face has 'withered'. He cannot forgive Tess: she is a different person. By day, he is controlled, but one night he sleepwalks. He decides on separation, and after visiting Talbothays, sends Tess home. Joan is typically vexed. Angel leaves for Brazil, having tried to take Izz with him. In October, Tess runs out of money and seeks work at Flintcomb-Ash with Marian. Visiting the Clares for news, she meets Cuthbert and his brother. Turning back, she hears a preacher. It is Alec.

### Who? What? Why? When? Where? How?
1    Felix and Cuthbert (44)
2    The man with the paint pot (44)
3    Losing courage before seeing the compassionate Clares (44)
4    Her past does not affect her love for him. She did not plan it. She is not the deceitful woman he is angry at (35)
5    Divorce, which is not in fact possible. Death (36)
6    He would despise himself or her: Alec, her 'husband in Nature' is still alive. Their children would find out and be ashamed (36)
7    He asks if she loves him more than Tess, and she says nobody could (40)
8    Hearing of his proposal to Izz, she feels threatened, and fears that her failure to make contact has seemed like indifference (43,44)
9    He is sullen and tyrannical. Angel knocked him down and Tess fled his advances (43)
10   Wet weather prevents her working. Her family need money. She needs winter clothes (41)

**Who is this?**

1 Angel (39)
2 Joan Durbeyfield (38)
3 Tess (42)
4 Mrs Clare (39)

**Where are we now?**

1 Talbothays: 'The gold of the summer picture was now gray' (37) Marlott: 'There was no place here for her now' (38)
2 Memories of Tess putting pressure on him, coinciding with Izz's visit (40)
3 Cold, wind, rain, later snow. Stony, chalky ground. Drab, featureless land. No trees. Contrast with 'green, sunny, romantic Talbothays' (42,43)
4 Groby: Trantridge, to town inn, to road, to Flintcomb-Ash (41,43). Marian and Izz: Talbothays to Flintcomb-Ash (43). Car Darch and sister: Trantridge to Flintcomb-Ash (43). Man with paint pot: Blackmoor Vale to Evershead (44). Alec: Trantridge to Evershead (44)

**Past and done?**

1 Tringham saw traces of d'Urberville family likeness in John Durbeyfield (1)
2 Angel relived his fight with the Trantridge man (Groby) in the inn in his sleep (33)
3 She was dressed by her mother for Alec (7) and by Angel at Wellbridge (34)
4 She lost courage on the brink of confessing to Angel on the way to the station (30)

**Open quotes**

1 '… he would have been the nobler man'
2 '… cruelty of lust and the fragility of love'
3 '… was yet the slave to custom and conventionality when surprised back into his early teachings'
4 '… this feminine loss of courage at the last and critical moment through her estimating her father-in-law by his sons'

**The woman pays**

Tess is rejected for a sin the man (Angel) dismisses (35). She is pestered and insulted, as an attractive fieldwoman (41). Marian, Retty and Izz have suffered in love (37). Izz suffers from Angel's fit of selfish rebellion (40). Women suffer exploitation as cheap labour (42)

# Self-test (Answers) Phase Six

**Uncover the plot**

Alec says religion was a 'jolly new idea' after his mother's death. Disturbed by Tess's looks, he makes her swear not to tempt him. Tess is turnip slicing when he appears at Flintcomb-Ash and asks her to marry him. Later, he breaks a preaching engagement and discusses religion with Tess. Alec blames Tess for his backsliding, and asks her to return to him: she hits him. He offers to help her family: tempted, she writes to Angel, who, meanwhile, feels 'love renascent'. Liza-Lu brings news that Joan is very ill. When John dies, the family are homeless. They go to Kingsbere, where Alec turns up again.

**Who? What? Why? When? Where? How?**

1 Marian and Izz (52)
2 Mr Clare to Alec (45) Tess to Angel: unsent (46), appealing (48), reproachful (51). Joan to lodging house at Kingsbere (52). Marian and Izz to Angel (52)
3 She is a deserted wife (46). Her mind is enslaved to Angel's (46). Alec has given more help than Angel (47)
4 Guilt at 'causing' his backsliding (47). Lost hope of Angel's return. Help for the family (51)
5 Disbelief in Providence/supernatural (46). Ethics ('religion of loving kindness'), not dogma (47)
6 Candlemas Fair, February (46). Lady Day, 6th April (52)
7 She is 'unsmirched', having refused 'resolutely' to stay 'at his pleasure' after her seduction (46)
8 Whimsical desire for a 'new sensation', being 'temporarily impressed' by his mother's death (46)
9 John has made no provision for the family (50). Joan leaves booking lodgings too late (52)
10 Shows how unimportant 'deviations from the social norm' are to a broad, experienced mind (49)

**Who is this?**

1 Angel (49)
2 The Durbeyfields (51)
3 Alec (47)
4 Tess (47)
5 The engine man (47)

**Before and after**

1 The Cross-in-Hand (45): crime, bargain with the devil, revenge, hanging. The d'Urberville coach (51): rape and murder, death to the one who hears it (as Tess just has)
2 Blow with a gauntlet, like her armed ancestors. She will draw blood again, killing Alec (47)
3 Tess hears coach. The family are heading for the vaults at Kingsbere. Tess strikes Alec for the second time. The man with the paint pot turns up again (51)
4 Return to Marlott: memories of the club-walking (50). Alec's offer of home in the poultry-house (45). The Kingsbere vaults John boasted of (52). Alec seducing Tess again (48)
5 Memories of Sorrow. Tess tells Alec about him (45) and tends his grave, to the village's disapproval (51). The children's faithful singing recalls his baptism (51)
6 Tess discussing him and his religious views. Passages at Emminster and Angel's development in Brazil. Recollection by Marian and Izz. Tess's hopes of his return. Letters sent to him
7 Crime associated with coach (51). 'Sir John's' vanity, and family's eviction as ancestors evicted others (50). Angel's acceptance (49). Decayed grandeur of tombs (52)
8 Exile of the 'better-informed class' of villagers to towns, their land put to more productive use (51). The brutalising, isolating effect of technology: the threshing machine (47,48)
9 (a) '... till she was a bygone herself'. (b) '... – the rhythm of change – alternate and persist in everything under the sky'. (c) '... changeth'

### Costume drama
A 'well-known form – so strangely accoutred as the Methodist' (45). 'A man in black... in a semi-clerical costume' (46). 'A person... dressed in a tweed suit of fashionable pattern' (47). 'A man in a long smockfrock' (50). 'A man in a white mackintosh' (51). 'A man on horseback' (52). A 'recumbent figure' on the d'Urberville tomb (52)

### Phased out
Tess (converted to scepticism by Angel – and de-converted from worship of Angel by Alec). Angel (converted from his view of Tess). Alec (converted by Mr Clare, and de-converted by Angel/Tess)

# Self-test (Answers) Phase Seven

### Uncover the plot
Angel returns to Emminster, looking ill. His parents give him Tess's second letter. He first writes to Marlott, but after a week's delay, he sets out to seek Tess. Tess is well remembered at Flintcomb-Ash, but Joan finally sends him to Sandbourne. He finds Tess as 'Mrs d'Urberville', dressed in grey-white. She says: 'It is too late': she is Alec's mistress. Later, Mrs Brooks finds Alec stabbed. Tess catches Angel at the high road and says: 'I owed it to you.' At last, 'tenderness' is 'absolutely dominant' in Angel. They rest at Bramshurst for a week, then flee to Stonehenge, where Tess is arrested. On a July morning, a black flag is raised, watched by Angel and Liza-Lu.

### Who? What? Why? When? Where? How?
1   Mrs Brooks, the landlady (56). The Bramshurst caretaker (58)
2   Liza-Lu. She will be looked after; she will be good for Angel; it will unite them in death (58)
3   Cuthbert is engaged to Mercy Chant (57)
4   His suffering appearance (53). His sensitivity to Tess (54,55). His acceptance of her past: paying for John's grave (54). His self-blame (53,55). His unconditional love (57)
5   Modern, artificial Sandbourne (55,56). Historic Wintoncester, in an ugly tower (59)
6   When the police close in (58). She is contented and distracted: perhaps hallucinating (57)
7   He has falsely made her give up her hope and trust in Angel, whom she has thus lost again (55,56). So that Angel would forgive her and love her again (57)
8   She fears her happiness and Angel's love cannot last, and will not face losing them (58)
9   Writing to Marlott. Trying Flintcomb-Ash (source of her last letter). Tracing Mrs Durbeyfield, via the new tenants in Marlott, and persuading her to tell him where Tess is (54)
10  John in a pretentious, unpaid-for grave. Joan as a respectable, almost dignified widow (54)

**Who is this?**
1    Liza-Lu, described by Tess (58)
2    Angel (57)
3    Joan Durbeyfield (54)
4    Tess (58)
5    Tess (58)

**This is your life**
1    The coach, and Tess's violent streak, has been a recurring theme, linked with Alec (47,51)
2    Angel is retracing Tess's journey, turning away from the Clares only to find Alec again (55)
3    Parson Tringham quoted this text in the first chapter
4    Tess was dressed up for Alec (7). He later promised her fine clothes (12). Angel dressed Tess in finery which then reminded him of the d'Urbervilles (35). Her 'fluty' voice first attracted Angel's attention to Tess (18)
5    Alec's blood dripped when Tess hit him (47). The colours red on white are Tess's motif
6    Angel had said: 'How can we live together while that man lives?' (36)
7    Tess was watched sleeping by Alec (11) and, with Angel, by the caretaker (58). She has often been 'self-sacrificing', and has seen herself as a victim in relation to Alec (48): he is now the 'victim' (57), echoing his own lying on a tomb (52)

**Familiar themes**
1    The past: Tess's personal past catching up at a place of communal past, older than her ancestral history
2    Nature: vast and ultimately indifferent, emphasised by the 'inappropriate' season (summer)
3    Fate: death is inevitable, carelessly destructive of the best of human values and emotions
4    Religion: the children sang 'In Heaven we part no more' (51), but Tess could no longer believe it. She is forced to share Angel's honest – yet comfortless – belief in humanity alone
5    Society: false 'Justice'. Fate: the 'President of the Immortals'. The past: the sleeping d'Urbervilles. Religion: instinctive prayerfulness of the watchers. Nature: life continues

**Phased out**
Alec fulfills the prophecy: 'I shall die bad'. Angel fulfills Tess's trust: protecting and loving her, and looking after Liza-Lu. Tess fulfills her destiny in killing Alec, claiming Angel as her true husband, and dying for her crime.

# ■ Writing an examination essay

## Take the following to heart

- *Carefully study each of the questions set on a particular text* Make sure you understand what they are asking for so that you select the one you know most about.
- *Answer the question* Obvious, isn't it? But bitter experience shows that many students fail because they do not actually answer the question that has been set.
- *Answer all the question* Again, obvious, but so many students spend all their time answering just part of a question and ignoring the rest. This prevents you gaining marks for the parts left out.

## The question

1  Read and understand every word of it. If it asks you to compare (the similarities) and/or contrast (the differences) between characters or events, then that is what you must do.
2  Underline all the key words and phrases that mention characters, events and themes, and all instructions as to what to do, e.g. compare, contrast, outline, comment, give an account, write about, show how/what/where.
3  Now write a short list of the things you have to do, one item under the other. A typical question will only have between two and five items at most for you to cope with.

## Planning your answer

1  Look at each of the points you have identified from the question. Think about what you are going to say about each. Much of it will be pretty obvious, but if you think of any good ideas, jot them down before you forget them.
2  Decide in what order you are going to deal with the question's major points. Number them in sequence.
3  So far you have done some concentrated, thoughtful reading and written down maybe fifteen to twenty words. You know roughly what you are going to say in response to the question and in what order – if you do not, you have time to give serious thought to trying one of the other questions.

## Putting pen to paper

The first sentences are important. Try to summarise your response to the question so the examiner has some idea of how you are going to approach it. Do not say 'I am going to write about the character of Macbeth and show how evil he was' but instead write 'Macbeth was a weak-willed, vicious traitor. Totally dominated by his "fiend-like queen" he deserved the epitaph "this dead butcher" – or did he?' Jump straight into the essay, do not nibble at its extremities for a page and a half. High marks will be gained by the candidate who can show he or she has a mind engaged with the text. Your personal response is rewarded – provided you are answering the question!

As you write your essay *constantly refer back to your list of points* and make sure you are actually responding to them.

## How long should it be?

There is no 'correct' length. What you must do is answer the question set, fully and sensitively in the time allowed. Allocate time to each question according to the percentage of marks awarded for it.

## How much quotation or paraphrase?

Use only that which is relevant and contributes to the quality and clarity of your answer. Padding is a waste of your time and gains not a single mark.